ABT

THE CHILD'S WORLD®

Encyclopedia of the
NFL

VOLUME THREE: Oakland Raiders >> Super Bowl XII

By James Buckley, Jr.
Jim Gigliotti
Matt Marini
John Wiebusch

KEY TO SYMBOLS

Throughout *The Child's World® Encyclopedia of the NFL*, you'll see these symbols. They'll give you a quick clue pointing to each entry's subject.

Active Coach **Active Player** **Football Term** **Hall of Fame** **Miscellaneous** **Stadium** **Super Bowl** **Team**

www.childsworld.com

Published in the United States of America by The Child's World®
1980 Lookout Drive, Mankato, MN 56003-1705
800-599-READ • www.childsworld.com

ACKNOWLEDGMENTS

The Child's World®: Mary Berendes, Publishing Director

Produced by Shoreline Publishing Group LLC
President / Editorial Director: James Buckley, Jr.
Designer: Tom Carling, carlingdesign.com
Assistant Editors: Jim Gigliotti, Matt Marini

Interior Photo Credits:
AP/Wide World: 9, 11, 12, 13, 15, 18, 24, 32, 34, 37, 62, 63, 78, 80, 83, 87-97; Corbis: 36, 54, 86;
Getty Images: 45, 50, 84. WireImage: 31, 83.
All other images provided by Focus on Football.
Icons created by Robert Pizzo.

LIBRARY OF CONGRESS CATALOG-IN-PUBLICATION DATA

The Child's World encyclopedia of the NFL / by James Buckley, Jr. ... [et al.].
    p. cm.
Includes index.
ISBN 978-1-59296-922-7 (v. 1 : alk. paper) – ISBN 978-1-59296-923-4 (v. 2 : alk. paper)
– ISBN 978-1-59296-924-1 (v. 3 : alk. paper) – ISBN 978-1-59296-925-8 (v. 4 : alk. paper)
1. National Football League–Encyclopedias, Juvenile. 2. Football–United States–Encyclopedias, Juvenile.
I. Buckley, James, 1963– II. Child's World (Firm) III. Title: Encyclopedia of the NFL.
    GV955.5.N35C55 2007
    796.332'64--dc22
                    2007005662

■ *Philadelphia's Chuck Bednarik*

S INCE ITS FOUNDING IN 1920, THE National Football League has played more than 12,000 games in 100 U.S. cities–and 10 countries. More than 17,000 players have strapped on their pads. They've combined to put up more than 400,000 points and score more than 45,000 touchdowns. That, my friends, is an awful lot of football!

In *The Child's World® Encyclopedia of the NFL*, we won't have room to include all of those players or recount all of those touchdowns. But we've put our helmets together and tried to give a complete picture of the very best and most important people, places, teams, and terms that football fans like you want to know more about.

You'll meet great members of the Pro Football Hall of Fame and read about today's top players. You'll relive some of the NFL's most memorable moments–from the Sneaker Game to the Coldest Game to the Greatest Game Ever Played. Need to learn how to "talk football"? These books will help you understand the terms and phrases you'll hear during a game. Finally, each of the NFL's 32 teams is covered with a complete history. All you'll need to enjoy these books is a love of football . . . and a knowledge of the alphabet!

■ *Michael Strahan*

Oakland Raiders

The Oakland Raiders started play in the American Football League in 1960, but the history of the Raiders really started in 1963, when Al Davis was named the head coach and general manager. In the decades since, no NFL team has been so deeply linked with one man, as Davis has molded the team in his own "outlaw" image. Along the way, the Raiders have won three Super Bowls and a legion of devoted, if somewhat colorful, fans.

Davis became the team's managing general partner in 1967, a title he still holds today (through 2006). The team won its first title that year, beating the Houston Oilers in the AFL Championship Game and moving on to face the Green Bay Packers in Super Bowl II. Led by quarterback Daryle "The Mad Bomber" Lamonica and a fabled deep passing attack, the Raiders made it to the next two AFL title games, too, but lost both.

After joining the NFL as part of the 1970 merger, the Raiders reached the Super Bowl again in the 1976 season. They defeated the Vikings 32-14 to win Super Bowl XI; receiver Fred Biletnikoff was the game's MVP. The head coach was John Madden, who would later become perhaps the NFL's most famous TV announcer as well as the namesake of the most popular football video game.

Former Patriots and 49ers quarterback Jim Plunkett led the Raiders to victory in Super Bowl XV in the 1980 season. Two years later, the team moved to Los Angeles. Its 1983 team was one of its all-time best, featuring superstars such as running back Marcus Allen, defensive end Lyle Alzado, and still led by an aging, but solid, Plunkett. The

■ *Marcus Allen was a graceful, speedy runner.*

Raiders dominated the competition in the playoffs, winning their two AFC games with ease and trouncing the Redskins 38-9 to win Super Bowl XVIII.

In 1989, the Raiders made former Oakland offensive lineman and Hall of Famer Art Shell the first African-American head coach in modern NFL history. The 1990s saw the Raiders post several winning seasons and earn playoff spots, but they didn't advance far in the postseason. In 1995, the Raiders made big news by deciding to move, back to the team's original home in Oakland.

Some of the great players who wore the Raiders' piratical logo include Hall of Fame linemen Shell, Gene Upshaw, and Jim Otto, who was called "Double Zero," after his unique uniform number; offensive stars such as receiver Tim Brown, tight end Todd Christensen, and running back Bo Jackson; and defensive stalwarts like cornerback Lester Hayes, linebacker Ted Hendricks, and defensive end John Matuszak.

The Raiders won the AFC West each year from 2000-02. Finally, Oakland returned to its championship form in 2002, winning the AFC title. In Super Bowl

■ *WR Randy Moss heads for the end zone.*

XXXVII, though, the club was trounced by the Buccaneers. In the seasons since then, the Raiders have sunk to new lows, posting records among the worst in the NFL.

The glory days of the Raiders are in the past, but their loyal and enthusiastic fans, sporting pirate costumes and the famous "Silver and Black," remain, as does Al Davis, Mr. Raider.

Davis's motto is "Commitment to Excellence." That motto has been lived up to at some points in Raiders' history, and might still be again someday.

OAKLAND RAIDERS

CONFERENCE: AFC

DIVISION: WEST

TEAM COLORS: SILVER AND BLACK

STADIUM (CAPACITY): McAFEE COLISEUM (63,132)

ALL-TIME RECORD: (THROUGH 2006): 421–319–11

NFL CHAMPIONSHIPS (MOST RECENT, INCLUDES AFL): 4 (1983)

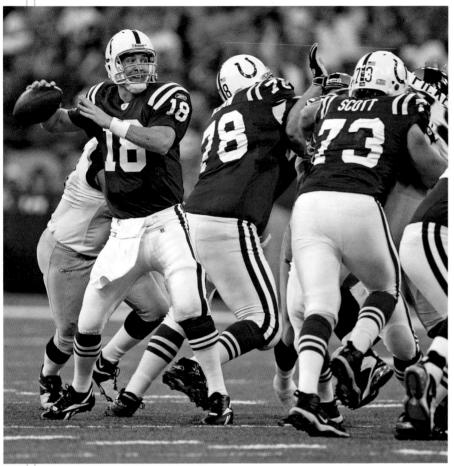

■ *The big bodies of the offensive line protect the quarterback.*

Offensive Coordinator

The coach on the team responsible for planning the plays his team's offense runs. He works with the head coach to choose the players for all offensive positions and to train those players in the team's plays. He creates the game plan for how his team will attack each opponent. Offensive coordinator is perhaps the second-most important coaching position. Coaches in this role often later move up to become head coaches.

Offensive Line

The five offensive players on the line of scrimmage closest to the football at the snap. The offensive line is made up of (from the quarterback's left) left tackle, left guard, center, right guard, and right tackle. The tight end can be part of the offensive line, and he can line up at either end.

The "O-line" is the primary blocking force for an offense. On run plays, the line tries to make holes for its runners to go through by shielding off opposing tacklers. On passing plays, the offensive linemen back up and form a pocket around the quarterback, giving him time to throw a pass.

Offense

The team in possession of the football. It is opposed by the defense. The offense starts the play at the line of scrimmage and tries to move the ball down the field. The defense is the team trying to stop the offense and also to take away the ball. The term also refers to the type of plays a team runs. For instance, a team that passes often has a "passing offense." A team that runs often might be called a "run offense."

NFL Officials

Referee: The referee is the crew leader and is in charge of all the officials and interprets any rules problems. During a play, he is positioned behind and to the side of the quarterback. His main responsibility is to watch the quarterback and the action around that position. When penalties are called, the referee announces the penalty to the crowd via a microphone.

Umpire: This is perhaps the most physically demanding position among officials. The umpire stands about five yards behind the defensive line, ready to call penalties committed along the line of scrimmage. His spot in the middle of the action means that he can find himself squashed between several players, though he does his best to avoid contact.

Head Linesman: This official stands at one sideline right on the line of scrimmage. He is looking for such penalties as offside or illegal motion. If a play goes to the sideline, he rules where the player went out of bounds. He also works with the chain crew, making sure they move the chains when appropriate.

Line Judge: This official stands on the opposite side of the field from the Head Linesman, looking for similar penalties on his side of the line of scrimmage. He also rules on out-of-bounds plays on his side of the field. The Line Judge also keeps the official time.

Field Judge: Farther up the field, about 20 yards from the line judge, is this official. His main job is to watch receivers who come into his area and make sure that they and the defenders follow the rules. When the ball comes into his area, he determines where a play ended.

Side Judge: Like the Field Judge, he stands about 20 yards upfield and pays closest attention to receivers and defensive backs.

Back Judge: Stands near the middle of the field about 25 yards from the line of scrimmage. He pays most attention to the tight end as that player moves down the field. The back judge helps rule on whether passes are legally caught. He also keeps track of the play clock.

■ *A side judge keeps a close eye on a play.*

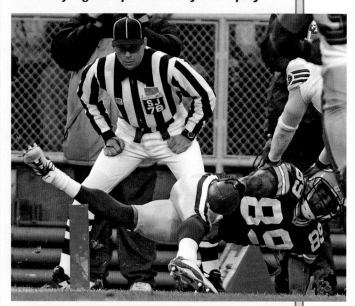

Offensive linemen must be very strong, durable, and quicker than you would think for players of their size. They take hits on every play, but they also must keep a sharp mind, because a missed blocking assignment on a play could easily end up costing his team yards or the ball, or lead to an injury. Left tackles, especially, are valued by coaches. In this position, the player is often the protector of the back side of a right-handed quarterback. Some left tackles are among the game's highest-paid players.

The center starts each play by snapping the football from the ground between his legs back to the quarterback. The center is also involved in calling signals that tell his teammates how to block on a particular play.

Officials

The seven men on the field during a game who enforce the rules and control the time of the game. NFL officials are hired by the league and assigned to "teams" that work together throughout a season.

The main job of all the officials to ensure that both teams follow the rules of the game. When they spot a rule being broken (a "penalty"), they throw a yellow flag (sometimes called a "penalty marker").

■ *Titans coach Jeff Fisher consults with a group of officials in their "zebra" stripes.*

■ *Few defensive linemen were as good for as long as durable and powerful Merlin Olsen (74).*

Olsen, Merlin

One of the most honored defensive linemen of all time, Olsen starred for the Los Angeles Rams from 1962-1976. He was part of the "Fearsome Foursome" defensive lines along with fellow Hall of Famer Deacon Jones, Lamar Lundy, Roger Brown, and Rosey Grier. He played college ball at the University of Utah, where he was named All-America and the winner of the Outland Trophy as the country's top lineman.

Olsen was a star from his first season. Strong, fast, and smart, he was named to the Pro Bowl as a rookie and would start in the all-star game for 14 consecutive seasons, an all-time best streak. He was named to the Pro Football Hall of Fame in 1982.

After his football career, Olsen worked as a football broadcaster and an actor. He had a long-running role on the TV series *Little House on the Prairie* and was well-known for appearing in commercials for a flower delivery service.

After the play is over, the official who called the penalty alerts the referee, who then reports the penalty to the teams and then to the stadium crowd (and the TV viewers) using a microphone. He also uses hand signals to show what the penalty was.

There are dozens of different rules that might be broken on any play, so officials are carefully trained to be ready for anything. NFL officials normally have many years of

■ *Big Jonathan Ogden looks for someone to block.*

a white hat while other officials typically wear black hats. Their striped shirts helped create one of the officials' well-known nicknames: zebras.

Though you might hear all NFL officials called "referees," only one member of the crew is the referee. The referee is in charge of the crew. Each of the seven officials on the field has a specific job and an area of the field he is responsible for. He usually works in that one area for at least a season, and some officials spend many years doing only one job.

The chart on page 7 lists the seven NFL officials and their duties.

Offsides

A penalty called when any part of a player's body is across the line of scrimmage before the ball is snapped. The ball is moved forward or backward five yards, depending on whether the offense or defense committed the foul.

Ogden, Jonathan

Left tackle has become one of the most important and highly paid positions in football. Left tackles are often most responsible for protecting the quarterback. One of the very best is Jonathan Ogden. Since joining the Baltimore Ravens in 1996 out of UCLA, Ogden has been a Hall-of-Fame caliber blocker. In 2006, he was chosen for his 10th consecutive Pro Bowl.

experience working in high school, college, and other pro leagues. Their work is reviewed by league executives, and all officials constantly review video of their work.

Though a game clock is used in the stadium for fans to see, the official time of the game is kept by the officials on the field. You might hear the referee instruct the stadium clock operator to adjust the time based on the officials' time.

Officials wear black-and-white shirts and white or black pants. The referee wears

Ogden's blocking helped the Ravens win Super Bowl XXXV. He has cleared the way for 1,000-yard rushers such as Jamal Lewis.

Listed at 6-9 and 345 pounds, Ogden is one of the biggest players at his position, but also one of the most nimble and athletic. Having signed a seven-year contract in 2004, Ogden figures to be among the best for several more years.

Onside Kick

A kickoff that is designed to give the kicking team a chance to recover the football. As soon as any kickoff goes 10 yards, it is a live ball and either team may recover. That usually doesn't matter, as the ball is boomed far downfield on regular kickoffs and the kicking team has no chance to get there before the receiving team.

Football ballet? No, just players going after an onside kick, which can be recovered by either team.

In an onside kick, however, the kicker gently kicks the ball so it goes only a short distance. The kicking team, lined up with the kicker, tries to race to the ball before the receiving team. Some kickers have perfected a way to make their kick bounce very high in the air, giving the kicking team time to run under the ball.

Onside kicks are not very successful, however. Kicking teams recover the ball only a small percentage of the time. Teams most often use them in desperate situations, such as when they trail in a game with little time left.

Oorang Indians

Though they only played for two seasons (1922-23) and managed to win just three games, the Oorang Indians remain one of the most interesting former NFL teams. Unlike most teams, which drew players from many places, the Indians were literally that: Indians. All the players were Native Americans. Owner Walter Lingo came up with the idea. He named it after his business, the Oorang Dog Kennels.

The most famous member of the team was one of the most famous athletes of all time: Jim Thorpe. A full-blood Sac and

■ *Otto was the AFL's only all-league center.*

Otto, Jim

Few NFL linemen have ever been as well-known or as good as long-time Oakland Raiders center Jim Otto. He was well-known among players and coaches for his outstanding blocking technique and leadership. He also became popular among fans for his unique uniform number. Taking a cue from his name, Otto wore the number 00. "Double Zero" helped the Raiders earn a spot in Super Bowl II in the 1967 seasons as the AFL champions. Otto was the only regular center the Raiders utilized for the team's first 15 years (1960-1974), playing in 210 straight games. He was an all-league pick 12 times and was named to the Hall of Fame in 1980.

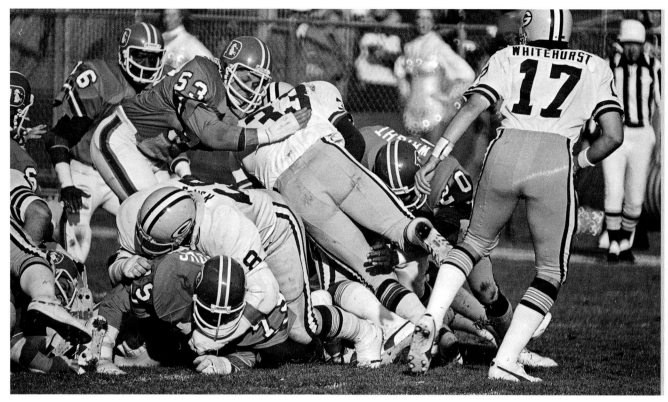

■ *The "Orange Crush" took its name from its uniforms, shown dark in this black-and-white photo.*

Fox tribe member, Thorpe was already a legend for winning Olympic medals in the pentathlon and the decathlon in 1912. He had also been a part of the founding of the NFL in 1920 and had played Major League baseball. Even with Thorpe, the Indians had little success, and Lingo closed the team down after two seasons.

Orange Bowl

Though not the home of an NFL team any longer, the Orange Bowl is one of football's most historic sites. The stadium was the home of the Miami Dolphins from their first season in 1966 until they moved to Dolphin Stadium in 1987.

Also, five Super Bowls, including two of the first three, were played in the stadium, located in Miami, Florida.

Opened in 1937, the 72,000-seat stadium was the home to an annual college football game named for it. The Orange Bowl game was played at the Orange Bowl stadium every year from then until 1996, when the game moved to what is now called Dolphin Stadium.

"Orange Crush Defense"

Nickname given to the defensive unit of the Denver Broncos during the 1970s, when the team rose from a decade of mediocrity to a period of success.

Owens, Terrell

An extremely talented wide receiver, Owens has gained as much notice for acting up as for scoring touchdowns. He joined the San Francisco 49ers in 1996 and spent eight years with the team. Though playing in the shadow of superstar Jerry Rice for part of this time, Owens made his mark with a stunning catch to win a 1997 playoff game against the Packers. In 2000, he set an all-time NFL record with 20 catches in a single game. His best year was 2001, when he caught 16 touchdown passes and racked up 1,412 receiving yards. In 2004, he moved to the Philadelphia Eagles and helped them reach Super Bowl XXXIX. Owens was injured several weeks before the game, and doctors felt he would not be able to play. Showing real determination, however, Owens battled back and played in the game, though the Eagles lost to the Patriots. He joined the Dallas Cowboys in 2006 and caught 13 more TD passes.

However, Owens' skills on the field are overshadowed by some unusual activities. A brash, outspoken, and occasionally selfish player, he once pulled out a pen after scoring a touchdown and autographed the ball. In a 49ers' game against the Cowboys, he once ran to the Dallas star logo at midfield and celebrated after scoring. He spoke out about his teammates, his quarterbacks, and about not getting thrown to often enough. He was once fined for spitting at an opponent and battled with 49ers' management over a contract before being traded to the Eagles. He was suspended by the Eagles before the 2005 season for arguing with coach Andy Reid. With 114 career touchdown catches (through 2006), Owens remains a talented player. His actions when not playing the game, however, make him a difficult teammate and employee.

■ *Owens has been a top receiver for three teams.*

Denver's colors are blue and orange, and fans took one of those colors and the name of a popular soft drink to create the de- fenses' popular nickname. Stars of the unit included linebackers Tom Jackson and Randy Gradishar and safety Louis Wright.

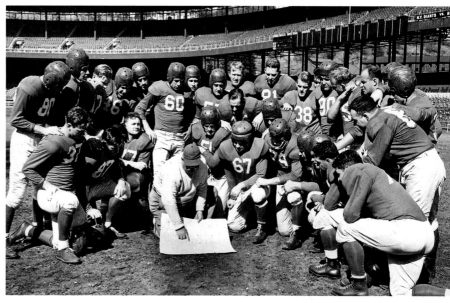

■ *"Okay, boys, here's the play." Owen, in cap, with his Giants.*

Out of Bounds

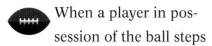 When a player in pos- session of the ball steps on or over the sideline or end line, he is out of bounds, and the play is over. He can also be tackled and knocked out of bounds. On NFL fields, the out-of-bounds territory is marked by a thick white line painted onto the grass or artificial turf.

Overtime

When a game is tied after 60 min- utes of regulation play, the two teams restart play in an overtime period. A new coin flip is held, and play begins with a kickoff and continues as usual. In sudden- death overtime, the first team to score any points wins the game.

During the regular season, just a single overtime period of 15 minutes is played. If neither team scores during that time, the game is declared a tie. During the playoffs, however, the teams play until one team scores. The longest such NFL overtime game was played in 1971, when the Dol- phins and Chiefs played for 82 minutes and 40 seconds (22 minutes and 40 seconds of overtime) before a field goal by the Dol- phins won the game.

Owen, Steve

First as a bruising running back and later as its longtime coach, Steve Owen was a part of the New York Giants from 1926 through 1953. He was named the player-coach in 1930 and became the full-time coach in 1933. As a coach, Owen led the Giants to victory in the 1934 and 1938 NFL Championship Games, as well as berths in six other NFL title games. Known for coaching his teams to have ferocious defenses, Owen was named to the Hall of Fame in 1966.

Page, Alan

Despite being just 225 pounds, Alan Page was one of the best defensive tackles of all time.

Page was a first-round pick of the Minnesota Vikings in 1967. He became a vital part of the Purple People Eaters defensive unit. Beginning in 1968, the Vikings won the NFC Central 9 times in 10 seasons, primarily due to the stifling defense led by

■ *Alan Page was a rare defender to be an MVP.*

Page. Four times, Page was selected the NFC defensive player of the year. The Vikings played in four Super Bowls during this era.

In 1971, Page became the only defensive tackle to be selected as the NFL MVP. Only one defensive player (linebacker Lawrence Taylor, 1986) has won the NFL MVP award since Page. He played in 218 consecutive games and 9 Pro Bowls. Page used his quick reflexes to recover 23 fumbles and block 28 kicks during his career. He retired after the 1981 season.

In 1978, the Chicago Bears signed Page. In his first full season with Chicago, the Bears posted their first 10-win season in 16 years, had the third-fewest points allowed, and reached the playoffs.

Page, who was born in Canton, Ohio, was inducted into Canton's Pro Football Hall of Fame in 1988. Today, Page, who attended Notre Dame, serves a judge on the Minnesota Supreme Court.

Pass

When a player, usually a quarterback, throws the ball downfield, it is considered a forward pass. The pass can be thrown either overhanded or underhanded, and does not necessarily have to cross the line of scrimmage to be a forward pass. That is, a pass can be made from the quarterback to another player who is behind the line of scrimmage.

Parcells, Bill

Bill Parcells retired after the 2006 season as the ninth-winningest coach in NFL history.

Parcells won 183 games in 19 seasons coaching the New York Giants, New England Patriots, New York Jets, and Dallas Cowboys. He was the first coach to lead four different franchises to the playoffs. The Giants won two Super Bowls (XXI and XXV) under Parcells' guidance, and he also led the Patriots to Super Bowl XXXI. He is one of only five coaches (Dan Reeves, Don Shula, Dick Vermeil, and Mike Holmgren) to have led two different franchises to a Super Bowl.

Perhaps the best example of Parcells' coaching ability is that he turned four struggling franchises into playoff teams. The Giants had just one winning season in 10 years prior to Parcells becoming head coach in 1983. The Giants reached the playoffs in his second year. The Patriots had four consecutive losing seasons when Parcells joined them in 1993. The Patriots also needed just two seasons to reach the playoffs.

The Jets had eight consecutive non-winning seasons prior to Parcells joining them in 1997. The Jets reached the playoffs in his second year. Dallas had three consecutive 5-11 seasons when Parcells joined in 2003, and he immediately led the Cowboys to the playoffs.

Parcells always coached his teams to have a strong running offense and a smart and hard-hitting defense.

■ *Parcells' last NFL stop was in Dallas.*

Teams can attempt only one forward pass per play. The passer must be behind the line of scrimmage when throwing a pass. If a player makes a pass from beyond the line of scrimmage, it's a penalty.

Passer Rating

The statistical system used to rate passers by game and season. The idea behind the system is the ability to compare passer ratings from one season to the next.

The passer rating uses four categories to compile its figure: percentage of completions per attempt; average yards gained per attempt; percentage of touchdown passes per attempt; and percentage of interceptions thrown. A mathematical formula combines these four numbers. The highest possible rating is 158.3. The best passer rating in history was turned in by Peyton Manning in 2004. Manning had a rating

Parker, Jim

One of the best offensive lineman in NFL history, Jim Parker could literally do it all.

Parker played both offensive and defensive line in college at Ohio State, and won the Outland Trophy as the nation's best lineman. The Baltimore Colts selected Parker in the first round in 1957 and immediately made him an offensive tackle. For five and a half seasons in Baltimore, he was one of the best in the game. Playing tackle, Parker handled the quick opposing defensive ends with his speed and agility.

In the middle of 1962, Parker was switched to guard. Parker once again proved his all-around ability, using his strength to keep opposing defensive tackles away from quarterback Johnny Unitas. Despite switching positions, Parker played in eight Pro Bowls.

■ Jim Parker set a new standard for offensive linemen.

The Colts won two NFL championships while Parker was on the offensive line, and the team never finished below .500 during his 11 seasons. Parker recalled coach Weeb Ewbank taught him one important rule early on, saying "'You can be the most unpopular man on the team if [Unitas] gets hurt.' How could I ever forget that?"

He became the first pure offensive lineman to be inducted into the Pro Football Hall of Fame. Parker was selected in his first year on the ballot (1973), and in 1994 was named to the NFL's 75th Anniversary All-Time Team.

of 121.1, which surpassed the previous mark of 112.8, set by San Francisco's Steve Young in 1994.

Pass Interference

The act of one player illegally denying another player the opportunity to catch a pass. A defensive player is not allowed to touch an offensive player who doesn't have the ball once the receiver is five yards downfield. The most common defensive pass interference is when a defender bumps or pulls on a receiver just before the ball arrives. The receiver, if he pulls or bumps the defender, can be called for offensive pass interference as well.

If the penalty is on the defense, it is a severe foul. The ball is placed at the spot of the foul (or a minimum of 15 yards), and the offense is given an automatic first down. If the penalty took place in the end zone, the offense gets the ball on the 1-yard line. If the offense commits the infraction, it is a 15-yard penalty.

Pass Pattern

A pass pattern is the route a receiver runs prior to catching a pass.

When coaches develop passing plays, they specify the distance and direction they want each player to run. For example, the wide receiver on the right side may run 10 yards, and then sharply cut toward the middle of the field, running directly across.

■ *A good pass rush can disrupt a quarterback.*

An exact route such as that is referred to as a pass pattern.

Marvin Harrison of the Indianapolis Colts is considered one of the best at precisely running his pass patterns.

Pass Rush

When the defense gets pressure on the quarterback while he is attempting to pass, it is referred to as a pass rush.

A strong pass rush usually either forces the quarterback to scramble or, if it succeeds, sacks him. The timing of the quarterback and offense can easily be disrupted with an active pass rush.

When a team has a strong pass rush, it usually helps the secondary as well. The quarterback may be hurried, and thus make an ill-advised pass into double coverage.

Passing Tree

The diagram shown below is known as a passing tree. It shows most of the basic pass patterns used in football. Teams might use different names for some of them or have slight variations, but these are the basics. A quarterback will tell each receiver on a play to run one pattern so that he

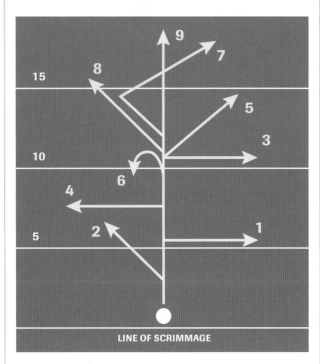

LINE OF SCRIMMAGE

■ *Though each team has its own playbook, football pass routes typically have names similar to these: 1: quick out; 2: slant; 3: deep out; 4: in route; 5: flag; 6: curl; 7: post corner; 8: post; 9: fly.*

knows where those receivers will be on the field after the snap.

PAT

This is an acronym (the initials) for Point After Touchdown (PAT), which is another way of describing an extra-point kick.

For a PAT, the ball is placed on the 2-yard line and is snapped back to the 10-yard line, where the kicker attempts to kick the ball through the uprights. If successful, the team is awarded one point.

A PAT is almost as automatic as any aspect of football. During the 2006 season, 99 percent of PAT attempts were success-ful. Jason Elam holds the NFL career re-cord by having made 371 consecutive PATs from 1993-2002.

Paul Brown Stadium

After 30 seasons of sharing River-front Stadium with baseball's Cincin-nati Reds, the Cincinnati Bengals moved into Paul Brown Stadium in 2000.

The Bengals' state-of-the-art facil-ity won the 2001 Merit Award from the American Institute of Architects. It was the first NFL stadium so honored. It had a grass surface for its first four seasons before switching to FieldTurf in 2004. Paul Brown Stadium features 132 suites and hosts 65,378 spectators.

The stadium is named for Paul Brown,

Payton, Walter

Considered one of the greatest running backs of all time, Walter Payton was a complete player.

Drafted by the Chicago Bears out of Division I-AA Jackson State in 1975, Payton led the league in kickoff return average his rookie year. In 1977, Payton led the league in rushes, rushing yards, rushing average, rushing touchdowns, and total touchdowns en route to being selected the NFL's MVP.

Against the Vikings in 1977, Payton rushed for a then-record 275 yards, a mark which stood for 23 years. From 1976-1986, he had at least 1,300 rushing yards in 9 of those 11 seasons.

Payton was a superb blocker and averaged 9.2 yards per reception for his career. He passed for eight touchdowns, an NFL record for most passing touchdowns by a non-quarterback.

After the 1987 season, Payton retired as the NFL's all-time leader in rushing yards (16,726 yards), yards from scrimmage (21,264 yards), and rushing touchdowns (110), though all those records have since fallen.

Payton was inducted into the Pro Football

■ *Payton's nickname was "Sweetness."*

Hall of Fame in 1993, his first year eligible. In 1994, Payton was one of the running backs on the NFL's 75th Anniversary All-Time Team.

Perhaps Payton's greatest honor came after his death in 1999. The NFL recognizes players for their on-field ability as well as their community service activities with the Walter Payton NFL Man of the Year Award.

who was the founder and first coach for the Bengals (1968) and the Cleveland Browns (1946). Brown was inducted into the Pro Football Hall of Fame in 1967.

Penalty

A penalty is when a player breaks a rule and he is noticed by an official on the field. When one of the seven offi-

■ The penalty marker is often called "the flag."

cials throws a yellow flag, it means there is a penalty.

A penalty can occur at any time during the game, whether or not the clock is moving. Penalties have even been called before a game (i.e., if a fight occurs, or a team is late arriving on the sideline).

Penalties can range from five yards to a pass interference penalty, in which the ball is placed at the spot of the foul. If a penalty is severe, the official can eject a player from a game.

Penalty Marker

 A penalty marker refers to a yellow penalty flag. When the official throws

his flag, it allows the players, crowd, and announcers to know an infraction has occurred. The penalty flag was first used in the NFL on September 17, 1948 in a game between the Boston Yanks and the Green Bay Packers. In 1965, the flag was changed from white to bright gold.

Pete Rozelle Award

The Super Bowl most valuable player, as selected by voters, is honored with the Pete Rozelle Award.

When Pete Rozelle retired as NFL Commissioner in 1989, the NFL renamed the Super Bowl MVP trophy in his honor. The first Pete Rozelle Award recipient was the New York Giants' Ottis Anderson, who was the MVP of Super Bowl XXV. Peyton Manning was the winner of the Super Bowl XLI Pete Rozelle Award.

The Pete Rozelle Award winner is chosen by a combination of votes from the media (80 percent) and fans (20 percent).

Philadelphia Eagles

Please see page 24.

Phil-Pitt Steagles

In 1943, the Philadelphia Eagles and Pittsburgh Steelers merged their teams for one season to form Phil-Pitt.

Due to the manpower shortage because of the fighting in World War II, the Cleveland Rams suspended operations for the

1943 season, leaving the NFL with nine teams. The Eagles and Steelers were both short-handed because of players joining the armed services. In June 1943, the NFL announced the Eagles and Steelers would

merge for one season. The "Steagles" divided their home games between the two cities, and the team's 1942 coaches, Earle (Greasy) Neale of Philadelphia and Walt

continued on page 26

Peppers, Julius

Julius Peppers, at the age of 27 in 2007, ranks as one of the best defensive players in football.

The Carolina Panthers selected Peppers with the second overall pick of the 2002 NFL Draft, and he immediately won the NFL defensive rookie of the year award. How important was Peppers' impact? The 2002 Panthers are the only defensive unit in NFL history to go from last in the league in defense (in 2001) to second in one season (2002).

He has shown his dominance by recording 13 games with at least two sacks. In six of those games, Peppers had three sacks. Peppers is not only strong, he is also fast. In 2004, his 203 combined return yards were the most by an NFL defensive lineman since the 1970 AFL-NFL merger.

Peppers has been selected as a starter for each of the past three Pro Bowls. He has registered 10-plus sacks in five of his six seasons. He owns club records for most sacks (53.5) and forced fumbles (17).

How good an athlete is Peppers? He played basketball at the University of North Carolina as a freshman and sophomore, and scored 21 points in an NCAA Tournament Game. But he gave up basketball and played only football as a junior before entering the NFL draft.

■ *Peppers is a rare mix of speed and strength.*

Philadelphia Eagles

Since head coach Andy Reid's arrival in 1999, the Eagles have been one of the NFL's most successful franchises. The Eagles played in four consecutive NFC Championship Games, and reached Super Bowl XXXIX in 2004 before losing 24-21 to New England. The Eagles have reached the playoffs six of the past seven seasons.

The Eagles' lone other Super Bowl experience was a 27-10 loss to the Oakland Raiders in Super Bowl XV, when Dick Vermeil guided a club led by quarterback Ron Jaworski, running back Wilbert Montgomery, and wide receiver Harold Carmichael.

Success did not always come so easily for the Eagles. The club began in 1933, and its nickname is taken from the symbol for President Franklin Delano Roosevelt's New Deal policy which helped America recover from the Great Depression.

The Eagles hit their stride in 1944, first by drafting running back Steve Van Buren. With Earle (Greasy) Neale as head coach, the Eagles played in three consecutive NFL Championship Games. After dropping the 1947 game, the Eagles won 7-0 in 1948 and 14-0 over the Cardinals the Rams in 1949.

■ *C/LB Chuck Bednarik was a force on offense and defense.*

PHILADELPHIA EAGLES

CONFERENCE: NFC

DIVISION: EAST

TEAM COLORS: MIDNIGHT GREEN, SILVER, BLACK, AND WHITE

STADIUM (CAPACITY): LINCOLN FINANCIAL FIELD (68,400)

ALL-TIME RECORD: (THROUGH 2006): 488-533-25

NFL CHAMPIONSHIPS (MOST RECENT): 3 (1960)

■ *QB McNabb is the field leader of the current Eagles.*

In 1960, the Eagles, coached by Lawrence (Buck) Shaw, defeated Vince Lombardi's Green Bay Packers. The 17-13 victory marked Lombardi's lone playoff loss of his entire NFL career. Quarterback Norm Van Brocklin and center/linebacker Chuck Bednarik were two of the key components to the Eagles' victory.

Unfortunately, both Shaw and Van Brocklin retired after the game, and the Eagles did not have another winning coach until Vermeil was hired in 1976. The club had moved into Veterans Stadium in 1971, and remained there until Lincoln Financial Field opened in 2003.

During the Veterans Stadium years, only three coaches, Vermeil, Buddy Ryan, and Rich Kotite, posted a winning record. Vermeil led the Eagles to the playoffs four consecutive seasons (1978-1981), including the franchise's first Super Bowl appearance. With Ryan, the Eagles posted three consecutive postseason appearances (1988-1990), but did not win a playoff game. Kotite had just one playoff team in four seasons.

With Reid at the helm, and Donovan McNabb at quarterback, Brian Westbrook at running back, and Brian Dawkins at safety, the Eagles are in position to make another run at the Super Bowl.

Kiesling of Pittsburgh, were co-coaches.

Phil-Pitt finished with a respectable 5-4-1 record, and finished just one game behind the Redskins and Giants in the NFL's Eastern Division. The Steagles split back into two teams after the season.

Pick Off (verb) or Pickoff (noun)

This is another way to describe an interception. Announcers will sometimes say a defender has "picked off" a pass, meaning he has intercepted the ball. The most "pickoffs" in one season was 14 by Dick (Night Train) Lane in 1952.

■ Ben Roethlisberger performs a perfect pitchout.

Pitchout

When a quarterback tosses the ball backwards to the running back, the play is called a pitchout. The pitchout is usually done underhanded, with two hands to ensure a quick and accurate delivery.

Pitchouts were very common prior to the 1950s, when teams used a lot of running plays. Today, the play is most common if the quarterback rolls out, pretending to run, only to then pitch the ball to the running back. The advantage for the offense is that the running back can catch a pitchout while running at full speed, whereas he has to be running a little slower to properly receive a handoff.

Pittsburgh Steelers

Please see page 28.

Plane of the Goal Line

The "plane of the goal line" is an invisible line that begins on the goal line and extends vertically up to the sky.

If a ball carrier "breaks the plane of the goal line" while maintaining possession of the football, the play is ruled a touchdown. The ball carrier does not have to actually land *in* the end zone. As long as the player has possession while the ball crosses the plane of the goal line, the play is ruled a touchdown.

Play Action

A play-action pass is when the quarterback fakes a handoff to the running back before throwing a pass downfield.

For a play-action pass to work well, the quarterback and running back must really "sell" the play to try to fool the defense. In other words, the quarterback may stick his arm completely out to fake the handoff. The running back must have his hands in position to grab the ball, and then run as if he is looking for a hole. This forces the linebackers and secondary to think a running play is occurring, only to have the quarterback then fire a pass downfield.

Play Clock

The play clock refers to the 40- or 25-second clock that runs in between every play.

When a play is completed, the play clock immediately starts. If the game clock has not stopped, the play clock allows 40 seconds between each play. If the game clock is stopped, then the play clock does not begin until the ball is marked by the official. In this situation, the offense has 25 seconds to run a play. If a team does not begin a new play before the time on the play clock runs out, a five-yard delay-of-game penalty is called.

One play clock is located at either end of the end zone, usually at eye level just to the right of the field-goal post.

■ *Playoff winners get the nicest trophies.*

Playoffs

The playoffs are a series of games played leading up to the Super Bowl.

In today's format, there are three rounds of playoffs. The Wild Card Playoffs include four games, two in each conference. The Divisional Playoff Games feature the four Wild-Card winners against the two teams with the best record in each conference. The four Divisional winners meet in the conference Championship Games. The two winners of the AFC and NFC championship games meet in the Super Bowl.

The very first playoff game was the 1933 NFL Championship Game, which

continued on page 30

Pittsburgh Steelers

They were the dominant team of the 1970s. The only franchise to win four Super Bowls in a six-year span (1974-79), the 1970s Pittsburgh Steelers are arguably the greatest dynasty in NFL history.

The dynasty began to come together when Chuck Noll was hired as head coach in 1969. His first draft pick, defensive tackle "Mean Joe" Greene, was the first of many fantastic draft choices made in six years. The 1969 draft also featured defensive end L.C. Greenwood. In 1970, quarterback Terry Bradshaw was the first overall pick, and the Steelers later added cornerback Mel Blount. In 1971, six future starters, highlighted by linebacker Jack Ham, entered the organization. Franco Harris was drafted in 1972 and, in 1974, the Steelers amazingly drafted linebacker Jack Lambert, center Mike Webster, and receivers Lynn Swann and John Stallworth.

In 1972, the Steelers won the first postseason game in the club's 40th sea-

■ *Bradshaw led the Steelers to four titles.*

son. Two years later, the Steelers throttled the Vikings 16-6 to win Super Bowl IX. To prove it wasn't a fluke, the Steelers repeated the next year, with a 21-17 win against the Cowboys. The Steelers won the AFC Central in 1976 and 1977, but failed to advance. The 1978 Steelers met the Cowboys in the Super Bowl again, winning 35-31. In 1979, the Steelers defeated the Los Angeles Rams 31-19.

In 1992, 35-year-old Bill Cowher was hired to replace Noll. Cowher promptly guided the Steelers to six consecutive postseason ap-

PITTSBURGH STEELERS

CONFERENCE: AFC

DIVISION: NORTH

**TEAM COLORS:
BLACK AND GOLD**

**STADIUM (CAPACITY):
HEINZ FIELD
(64,350)**

**ALL-TIME RECORD:
(THROUGH 2006):
531-510-21**

**NFL CHAMPIONSHIPS
(MOST RECENT):
5 (2005)**

pearances, highlighted by a trip to Super Bowl XXX. The Steelers lost two AFC Championship Games at home until 2005, when Pittsburgh won three consecutive road games to reach Super Bowl XL. Playing the Seattle Seahawks, the Steelers won a hard-fought game 21-10 for the franchise's fifth Super Bowl title. The Steelers' Super Bowl wins are matched only by the 49ers and Cowboys.

The Steelers, owned by the Rooney family since Art Rooney became the founder and owner in 1933, had just seven seasons with a winning record in the franchise's first 40 years. In the 35 years since, the Steelers have had just seven losing seasons.

In 2006, former Minnesota Vikings' defensive coordinator Mike Tomlin was hired by Art's son Dan as Cowher's replacement. With a strong team—featuring Troy Polamalu, Hines Ward, and Ben Roethlisberger—Pittsburgh is are ready to continue their winning ways in the Steel City.

■ *The Steelers have long been known for their outstanding defensive teams.*

pitted the Western Division-champion Chicago Bears against the Eastern Division champion New York Giants. The Bears won 23-21. One Wild-Card tam–the non-division winner with the best record–from each conference was added to the playoffs in 1970. Two Wild-Card teams from each conference beginning in 1978, and three in 1990. The current format used in the NFL playoffs began in 2002.

■ *Polamalu: Long on hair, long on talent*

Pocket

The area directly behind center where the quarterback stands as he looks downfield to throw the ball. Once a quarterback rolls out beyond where the tackle lined up, he is considered "outside the pocket."

When announcers say a quarterback is "flushed from the pocket," it means he must roll out or scramble to get away from the pass rush. The pocket is formed by the surrounding offensive linemen, who move backward at the snap to block defenders and protect the quarterback.

Point After Touchdown

See PAT.

Politicians (Former NFL Players in Politics)

After their playing career is over, several NFL players have pursued careers in politics.

Among former NFL players, perhaps the two most famous politicians are Jack Kemp and Steve Largent. Kemp, who played quarterback and led the Buffalo Bills to two AFL titles, was a New York Congressman, a member of the Cabinet, and a 1996 vice-presidential nominee. Largent, a Pro Football Hall of Fame wide receiver, was in Congress for seven years representing a district in Oklahoma and later a candidate for governor.

Pollard, Fritz

 Fritz Pollard is one of the true pioneers of the NFL.

Pollard was one of just two African-American players in the APFA (later re-named NFL) in 1920. With Pollard serving as one the league's best running backs, the Pros had an 8-0-3 record and were crowned as the league's first champions.

The following year, Pollard was named the co-coach of the Akron Pros, making him the league's first African-American head coach. Pollard coached and played for four franchises through 1926.

For his contributions on and off the field, Pollard was inducted into the Pro Football Hall of Fame in 2005.

■ *Hall of Fame QB/coach Fritz Pollard*

Another high-profile ex-NFL player was former U.S. Supreme Court justice Byron "Whizzer" White. President Gerald Ford was not in the NFL, but was a star player at the University of Michigan.

The most recent politician with NFL ties is former Redskins and Saints quarterback Heath Shuler. He was elected to the House of Representatives in 2006.

Polamalu, Troy

Pittsburgh Steelers safety Troy Polamalu may have been the best player in football during the 2005 postseason.

As the Steelers won four games en route to the Super Bowl XL title, Polamalu did it all for the defense. He intercepted a pass and registered a half sack in their first victory, and proceeded to register 24 tackles in the postseason.

Known as much for his long, flowing hair as for his on-field ability, Polamalu was originally a first-round draft pick from Southern California in 2003. He was selected as the Steelers' top rookie that season, and was voted to the Pro Bowl each of the past three seasons (2004-06). He is regarded as one of the game's best safeties.

■ *This photo shows the Polo Grounds set up for baseball.*

Polo Grounds

The Polo Grounds, a famous stadium located in New York City, served as the home field for three different professional football teams.

The Polo Grounds opened for baseball in 1911 and was the first home for football's New York Giants in 1925. The Giants played in the Polo Grounds for 31 years. In 1949, the NFL's New York Bulldogs played at the Polo Grounds in their only season of existence. Beginning in 1960, the New York Titans, who later became the Jets, played four seasons at the Polo Grounds. In 1963, the Jets were the last professional team to play a game in the stadium.

Along with football, the Polo Grounds also served as the long-time home of the baseball New York Giants, and was the home for a few seasons for baseball's Yankees and Mets, as well.

The Polo Grounds stadium was built on the site of what was actually a field used for polo, though the stadium was never used for that sport.

Pontiac Silverdome

Located in Pontiac, Michigan, just outside of Detroit, the Pontiac Silverdome was the home for the Detroit Lions for 27 seasons. After 40 seasons playing outside at Tiger Stadium, the Lions moved into the Pontiac Silverdome in 1975. It opened the same season as the Louisiana Superdome, making them the second and third domed stadiums. Prior to 1975, the only domed stadium was the Astrodome in Houston. With a capacity of more than 80,000, the Pontiac Silverdome was one of the largest stadiums in the NFL.

In January 1982, the 49ers and Bengals played Super Bowl XVI in the Pontiac Silverdome. In 2002, the Lions moved to Ford Field. The Pontiac Silverdome served as the practice site for the Steelers prior to Super Bowl XL, which was held at Ford Field.

The NBA's Detroit Pistons played in the Pontiac Silverdome from 1978-1988. Many concerts and events are still held there.

Porter, Joey

A three-time Pro Bowl linebacker, Joey Porter is among the elite linebackers in the NFL. Porter ranks fourth in Pittsburgh Steelers' history with 60 career sacks. He was the Steelers' defensive co-MVP in 2002, and he played in the Pro Bowl following the 2001, 2002, and 2005 seasons.

Porter began his career with the Steelers in 1999 out of Colorado State. In his second season, Porter burst open the scene, registering 10.5 sacks and starting every game. Porter just turned 30 years old in March 2007, when he signed a $20 million contract to join the Miami Dolphins and add to his already-outstanding record as a linebacker.

Possession

This most commonly refers to whether or not a player has "possession" of the ball before hitting the ground. When a ball carrier is being tackled, he must maintain possession until hitting the ground. If a player is trying to catch a thrown pass, he must have a secure grip of the ball before he is tackled. In either case, this means that he holds on to the ball without dropping it or losing control of it.

Another definition of "possession" is which team's offense is on the field, meaning that a team, rather than just a player, has possession of the ball.

Pottsville Maroons

The Pottsville Maroons, located approximately 100 miles northwest of Philadelphia in Pottsville, Pennsylvania, nearly won the NFL championship in their first season in 1925.

The Maroons, an extremely successful independent team, joined the NFL that year and finished with a 10-2 record. The Chicago Cardinals played two extra games and posted an 11-2-1 record and, even

■ *Porter earned three Pro Bowl selections with Pittsburgh.*

■ *This kicking shoe, bronzed for display, was used by the Maroons.*

though the Maroons beat the Cardinals 21-7, Chicago was declared NFL champions. The Maroons were even suspended from the NFL for playing an illegal exhibition game late in the season, but were welcomed back in 1926. That year, the Maroons had another excellent season, finishing in third place with a 10-2-2 record.

The Maroons struggled the next two seasons, and moved to Boston and played as the Boston Bulldogs in 1929. After a 4-4 record that season, the club folded.

Preseason

Preseason football games are games played prior to the season. Most are played in the month of August. Each NFL team plays at least four preseason games. These games allow veteran players to get prepared for the upcoming season. It also allows teams to play younger players and find out how they perform in game situations. Statistics from preseason games do no count in a player's career record. In fact, most veteran players appear only briefly in preseason games.

Prevent Defense

The Prevent Defense is one of the most controversial strategies in football. The Prevent Defense refers to a type of defense played by a team, usually when it has a lead late in a game. When the team on defense is winning, it may stop pressuring the quarterback and drop its secondary into a deep zone. The idea, from the defense's perspective, is to not allow a team to complete long passes. However, if a team is playing the Prevent Defense, the quarterback usually has more time to scan the field and find an open receiver.

Critics of the Prevent Defense say it "prevents victories" because it allows offenses to move downfield with ease, whereas the offense may have been struggling to move the ball up until that point in the game. For this reason, using the Prevent Defense is one of the most controversial decisions in football.

Pro Bowl, The

The NFL's All-Star Game is called the Pro Bowl. It is always the final game of the NFL season.

Played one week after the Super Bowl, the Pro Bowl has been played in Honolulu, Hawaii, since January 1980. The game consists of the best players from the AFC against the NFC's best players. The rosters are chosen by a combination of voting conducted by players, coaches, and fans.

The first Pro Bowl game was played in January 1939. The first five Pro Bowl games featured the NFL champion against a team of all-stars from the rest of the league. The format of players from different divisions playing against each other started after the 1950 season, and the AFC-NFC Pro Bowl began after the 1970 season.

Pull

If an announcer refers to the word pull during a running play, it usually refers to a "pulling guard."

A pulling guard loops around the center and runs in front of a ball carrier, blocking anyone who gets in his way. For example, if the plan is for the running back to run to his right, the left guard, when the ball is snapped, immediately cuts between the center and quarterback. The left guard then gets to the running back's path and turns his shoulders upfield so he can place a solid block on any defender.

This offensive play was made famous by Vince Lombardi's Green Bay Packers of the early 1960s. Guard Jerry Kramer perfected the play for the Packers.

Punt

A punt is usually a high-arcing kick by the punter. Teams punt when it is fourth down and they are forced to return the ball to the other team.

A good punt can help in the battle of field position, too. If a punter can pin a team deep in its own territory, it becomes more difficult for the opposing offense to drive to the end zone.

■ *Each conference wears new Pro Bowl uniforms.*

Punter

The punter is the player who comes into the game, almost exclusively on fourth down, and kicks the ball downfield.

The punter stands approximately 15 yards behind the line of scrimmage. He catches the ball and then takes a step or two before booming the ball high downfield. The higher a punter kicks the ball, the better the likelihood that his defense can get downfield and be in position to stop the punt returner.

A player who only punted has never been inducted into the Pro Football Hall of Fame. In 1994, Oakland Raiders punter Ray Guy was chosen as the punter for the NFL's 75th Anniversary All-Time Team.

Punt Returner

When the offense decides to punt the ball, most commonly on fourth down, the defensive team sends one player deep to receive the punt. The punt returner usually stands 40 yards downfield. When he

Pro Football Hall of Fame

Located in Canton, Ohio, the site of the original organizational meeting in 1920, the Pro Football Hall of Fame opened in 1963. It contains five buildings and is 82,307 square feet of football history, highlights, plaques, and memorabilia. Nearly eight million fans have visited the Pro Football Hall of Fame.

The Hall of Fame's main building has a unique shape. The main building has a tall, pointed roof designed to look like a football.

Each year, anywhere from four to seven people can be elected by a vote of a committee of media members.

A complete list of the 241 Hall of Fame members (through 2007) can be found beginning on page 98.

■ *The Hall of Fame building includes displays on football history.*

catches the ball, he attempts to return the punt toward his end zone. Before he catches the ball, if the punt returner decides he has no room to return the punt, he may call for a "fair catch." This allows him to catch the ball without being tackled, but he cannot advance it.

Billy (White Shoes) Johnson, who played for three teams in the 1970s and 1980s, is the punt returner on the NFL's 75th Anniversary All-Time Team.

"Purple People Eaters"

In the 1960s and 1970s, the Minnesota Vikings'

■ *The punter (1) has no chance against speedy punt returner Devin Hester.*

defensive line was known as the "Purple People Eaters." The nickname stems from the Vikings' purple home uniforms and the pure strength and size of the defensive front four, which would devour or "eat" ball carriers. It was also the title of a popular song.

During this era (1968-1977), the Vikings won nine division titles in ten seasons. Seven times in those ten seasons, the Vikings ranked in the top three in fewest points allowed.

The main Purple People Eaters were defensive ends Carl Eller and Jim Marshall, along with tackle Alan Page. The second defensive tackle was a combination of Gary Larsen (1968-1973) and Doug Sutherland (1974-77).

Pylon

Each end zone has four orange pylons, which are short, foam rectangles. They are located at the four corners of the rectangular end zone.

When running toward the end zone, if the ball carrier reaches out and touches the ball with the pylon, he is awarded a touchdown.

Qualcomm Stadium

The home of the San Diego Chargers since the stadium opened in 1967, Qualcomm has had several names. Until 1980, it was simply San Diego Stadium. That year, local sportswriter Jack Murphy passed away. It had been Murphy who had inspired the city to build the stadium for its local football team. To honor him, it was renamed for him, becoming San Diego Jack Murphy Stadium. Major renovations in 1984 and again in 1997 increased seating capacity to 70,000. After the 1997 additions, the communications company Qualcomm paid $18 million to have the stadium named for it.

■ *Donovan McNabb strikes a classic quarterback pose.*

Quarter

An NFL game is divided into four equal parts of 15 minutes each. Each of these 15-minute periods is called a quarter. Thus the game includes the first, second, third, and fourth quarters.

Quarterback

The quarterback is the most important position on the offensive team and perhaps one of the most difficult jobs in pro sports. Quarterbacks receive the ball to start nearly every offensive play. They take the ball and hand it off or toss it to a back or they throw a forward pass to a receiver. A quarterback's success at these tasks often means the difference between victory and defeat.

Quarterbacks are also seen as leaders by their teams, fans, and coaching staffs. Their attitudes can inspire a team to achieve great things. A bad attitude or a display of indecision, on the other hand, can have a very negative effect on a team.

Why the name quarterback? Football teams didn't always have such a position. There were fullbacks and halfbacks in the earliest formation. Halfbacks usually got the ball and simply ran with it. There were fewer handoffs and no passes. As ideas such as the T-formation began to take hold, a

■ *Two large decks of covered seats loom over the turf at Qwest Field.*

new position was needed to start the plays and pass the ball. By the 1940s, the quarterback was cemented as the key position on offense, and players at that position were the biggest stars . . . and commanded the highest salaries.

In those early days, quarterbacks also called all of a team's plays. More recent quarterbacks listen to a helmet radio as a coach decides what play the quarterback will call. The quarterback still has to have his team's entire playbook memorized, and he must know what every member of his team will do on every play. He can also change the play using hand and voice signals just before the snap of the ball; this is called an "audible."

The pressure on quarterbacks is enormous. The very best quarterbacks combine great physical skill with mental toughness to overcome this pressure. The less-successful quarterbacks succumb to this pressure.

Qwest Field (Seattle)

Located alongside Puget Sound in downtown Seattle, Qwest Field is home to the Seattle Seahawks. The stadium opened in 2002 and was given its present name in 2004 after a communications company paid for the naming rights. The stadium has a unique roof structure that covers 70 percent of the seats, but still leaves the field open to the elements. Qwest was the site of the 2005 NFC Championship Game, won by the Seahawks on their way to Super Bowl XL (which they lost to Pittsburgh). The stadium seats 67,000 fans and has an FieldTurf playing surface.

Ralph Wilson Stadium

 Ralph Wilson Stadium has been the home of the Buffalo Bills since 1973. The stadium is located in Orchard Park, New York, which is several miles outside of Buffalo. The stadium seats 73,967 fans and has an artificial playing surface. For the first 25 years of its existence, the venue was known as Rich Stadium (after the Rich Products Corporation). In 1999, it was re-named after the Bills' founder and owner.

The Bills earned three of their record four consecutive trips to the Super Bowl from 1990 to 1993 in conference title games played at the stadium. It also was the site of the greatest comeback in NFL history. Buffalo trailed the Houston Oilers 35-3 in a 1992 AFC Wild-Card Playoff Game before winning 41-38 in overtime.

Many fans who had left the game in the third quarter hurried back into the stadium as the Bills rallied.

Before moving into their current home, the Bills played at War Memorial Stadium in Buffalo. (That stadium later was used in the baseball motion picture, *The Natural*.)

Raymond James Stadium

 The Tampa Bay Buccaneers have played their home games at Raymond James since the stadium opened in the 1998 season. It is a 65,657-seat, natural-grass facility. At one end of the field sits a 103-foot replica of an 1600s pirate ship; its cannons fire when the Bucs score!

In January of 2001, Raymond James Stadium was the site of Super Bowl XXXV between Baltimore and the New York Giants. The Ravens won, 34-7. The stadium also is scheduled to host Super Bowl XLIII in the 2008 season.

Raymond James Stadium is not named after an individual person. Instead, it is the name of one of the largest investment firms in the United States. Its headquarters are in St. Petersburg, Florida.

RCA Dome

The RCA Dome is the home of the Indianap-

■ *You can see the orange pirate sail behind the far end zone.*

olis Colts. The indoor stadium seats 55,506 fans and has an artificial playing surface. The stadium originally was called the Hoosier Dome before RCA purchased the naming rights in 1994.

In addition to hosting NFL games, the RCA Dome has been a popular site for other sporting events, such as NCAA basketball tournament games, as well as conventions and trade shows.

The Colts have played in the dome since moving to Indianapolis from their original home Baltimore in time for the 1984 season. Construction on a new stadium with a retractable roof began in 2005. The team planned to move into the new facility by the 2008 season.

■ *Home of the Colts: action from inside the RCA Dome*

Realignment

Realignment means to change the way things or groups work together. In the NFL's case, that means changing how its teams are organized into divisions or conferences. The league often has tinkered with its groupings, but its most important realignment efforts came in 1933, 1967, 1970, and 2002.

In 1933, the league split into two divisions (Eastern and Western) for the first time, thus creating an end-of-season championship game. The champions of

each division played in the title game. Previously, the league title was awarded to whatever team had the best record. There were no playoffs.

In 1967, when the NFL expanded to 16 teams, it created four divisions that were organized into Eastern and Western Conferences. That meant there was a round of playoffs among division winners before the championship game.

When the AFL-NFL merger officially took effect in 1970, realignment created today's American Football Conference (AFC) and National Football Conference (NFC). The 10 AFL teams were joined by

The NFL's most recent realignment came when the league expanded to 32 teams in 2002. The teams were organized into eight divisions of four teams each, with four divisions in each conference. The playoffs remained at 12 teams: eight division winners, plus two wild-card teams from each conference.

Red Zone

The red zone is the area on the field from the 20-yard lines down to the goal lines in the defensive team's end of the field. It's not an official designation, but lots of times you'll hear players, coaches, and television announcers talk about the importance of scoring points once an offense moves the ball into the red zone.

The best NFL teams often are the ones that take the most advantage of their opportunities in the red zone. On defense, the best teams prevent their opponents from scoring touchdowns inside the 20-yard line.

Reed, Ed

Safety Ed Reed is the Baltimore Ravens' all-time leading interceptor and a former Associated Press NFL defensive player of the year. He is one of those players who always seems to be around the ball. He picked off five passes in 2006 to raise his five-year career total to 27.

■ *Safety Ed Reed is a ballhawk for the Ravens.*

three established NFL teams to form the 13-team AFC; the remaining 13 established NFL teams became the NFC. The two conferences each had three divisions. The division champions plus one wild-card team—the team with the best record among the non-division winners—made the playoffs. (A second wild-card team from each conference was added in 1978, and a third in 1990.)

Reed's best season came in 2004, when he led the NFL with nine interceptions and earned his defensive player of the year award. He returned one of his thefts 106 yards for a touchdown in a game against Cleveland. It was the longest interception return in NFL history. His 358 total yards on interception returns that season was another league mark.

Reed made the Pro Bowl for the third time in his career in 2006.

Referee

The referee is the man in charge of the officiating crew. He interprets any rules problems. During a play, he is positioned behind and to the side of the quarterback. His main responsibility is to watch the quarterback and the action around that position. When penalties are called, the referee announces the penalty to the crowd via a microphone. He also uses hand signals to show what the penalty was. (See "NFL Officials" on page 7.)

Reliant Stadium

Reliant Stadium is a retractable-roof stadium that is the home of the Houston Texans. A retractable roof means that it can be left open or kept closed depending on the weather. Certain rules apply to when it can be opened or closed. (For instance, if a game begins with the roof closed, it must remain closed.)

Reliant Stadium opened in 2002. It has a grass playing surface and a seating capacity of 71,054. The stadium was the site of Super Bowl XXXVIII in the 2003 season. New England defeated Carolina in that game, 32-29.

Reverse

A reverse is a type of running play designed to trick defenses that are especially quick to chase after the ball carrier

continued on page 45

■ *Officials, like this referee, have uniform numbers, too.*

Rice, Jerry

Jerry Rice is usually considered the greatest wide receiver in NFL history. He played 20 seasons from 1985 to 2004, most of it for the San Francisco 49ers. He is the league's all-time record holder for career catches (1,549), receiving yards (22,895), and touchdown receptions (197), leading all categories by a wide margin. He holds all those records for the postseason, too. And his 208 total touchdowns (including 11 on rushes or returns) is another NFL record.

Rice was the 16th overall choice in the 1985 draft by the 49ers, who traded two picks to the New England Patriots in order to move up and pick him. He had 927 receiving yards as a rookie that year, then posted 11 consecutive seasons of 1,000 or more yards catching passes. That included 1,848 yards in 1995, which still is the most in a season in NFL history.

Rice's work ethic and durability were as legendary as his play on the field. He played in every game in 18 of his 20 NFL seasons, missing time only because of a knee injury in 1997 (14 games) and the players' strike in 1987 (three games). Despite the strike, though, he still set an NFL record by catching 22 touchdown passes in only 12 games in '87.

Rice earned 13 Pro Bowl selections in his career and played on four 49ers' teams that won the Super Bowl. He was named the MVP of San Francisco's 20-16 victory over Cincinnati in game XXIII after catching 11 passes for 215 yards. The incomparable Rice is certain to be inducted into the Pro Football Hall of Fame in his first year of eligibility in 2010.

■ *Rice was a San Francisco treat.*

An effective reverse looks like a normal running play at the beginning. A running back takes a handoff or pitch (a backward toss) and begins running toward one side of the field. Instead of turning upfield, though, he hands off or pitches the ball to another player (usually a wide receiver) who is running in the opposite direction.

RFK Stadium

The Washington Redskins played their home games in RFK Stadium for 36 seasons from 1961 to 1996. The stadium originally was known as D.C. Stadium. It was renamed after Senator Robert F. Kennedy was assassinated while campaigning for President in 1968.

The Redskins won all five NFC Championship Games that they hosted at RFK Stadium (all of those title games came between the seasons of 1972 and 1991). Washington went on to win the Super Bowl three of those years. During those years, RFK was often filled to capacity with some of the NFL's most devoted fans; some even dressed up like those pictured.

Before moving into RFK Stadium, the Redskins played at Griffith Stadium from 1937 to 1960. In 1997, they moved to their current home at FedExField (originally called Jack Kent Cooke Stadium). In 2005, baseball's Washington Nationals began playing their home games in RFK Stadium after moving from Montreal.

■ *These Redskins fans dressed as "The Hogs."*

Rice, Simeon

Simeon Rice is a three-time Pro Bowl defensive end who has amassed more than 100 sacks in an NFL career that began in 1996.

Arizona chose Rice with the third overall pick of the '96 draft. He amassed 51.5 sacks in five seasons with the Cardinals, including a career-best 16.5 sacks in 1999. In 2001, Rice signed with Tampa Bay and proved to be one of the final pieces to the club's championship puzzle. He had an NFC-leading 15.5 sacks in 2002 as the Buccaneers' dominating defense carried them to a Super Bowl championship.

■ *Simeon Rice (97) is one of the NFL's top pass rushers.*

Riverfront Stadium

The Cincinnati Bengals played their home games at Riverfront Stadium from 1970 through the 1999 season. They moved into their current home (Paul Brown Stadium) in 2000.

Riverfront Stadium was a multipurpose stadium that not only housed the NFL's Bengals, but also Major League Baseball's Cincinnati Reds. The Bengals won a pair of AFC Championship Games (1981 and 1988) at the site. The 1981 game, a 27-7 victory over the Chargers, was notable for its freezing temperatures. It was minus-9 degrees at kickoff, with a wind-chill factor of minus-59.

In 1996, Riverfront was renamed Cinergy Field after the Cincinnati energy company purchased the naming rights. The stadium was demolished in 2002.

Rice concluded his sixth season with Tampa Bay in 2006. His 121 career sacks at the close of the year ranked second only to the Giants' Michael Strahan (132.5) among active NFL players.

Rice Stadium

Rice Stadium is a college football stadium that also has hosted a Super Bowl, an AFL All-Star Game (in January of 1966), and Houston Oilers' home games from 1965 to 1967.

In the lone Super Bowl played at the site, the Miami Dolphins beat the Minnesota Vikings 24-7 in game VIII in the 1973 season. The stadium remains the home of the Rice University Owls' football team.

Roethlisberger, Ben

The Pittsburgh Steelers' Ben Roethlisberger is the youngest quarterback ever to lead his team to a victory in the Super Bowl. Roethlisberger was just 23 years old and in his second NFL season when his Steelers beat the Seattle Seahawks 21-10 in Super Bowl XL in 2006.

A former star in college at Miami of Ohio, "Big Ben" was drafted by the Steelers with the 11th pick in 2004. He came off the bench when starter Tommy Maddox was injured in the second game of his rookie year and went on to lead Pittsburgh to 14 wins in a row. The Steelers eventually lost to New England in the AFC Championship Game that year, but they returned to play for the conference title again in 2005. That time, they beat Denver as Roethlisberger passed for two touchdowns and ran for another score, earning the Steelers a spot in the Super Bowl.

Pittsburgh relied on its young quarterback to throw the ball more often in 2006. After recovering from injuries suffered in a motorcycle accident, he established personal bests with 3,513 yards passing and 18 scoring tosses that year. But the defending champs won only eight games and missed the playoffs for the first time in Roethlisberger's young career.

Rollout

A rollout refers to the action of a quarterback who moves to one side of the field or the other as he prepares to pass. This is different from the quarterback's usual drop, which is straight back as the offensive linemen form a pocket of protection around him (see "pocket").

A rollout generally is used to keep the quarterback away from a specific area of pressure from the defense. It also can be used, though, to give the quarterback the option to run or pass the ball depending on what the defensive players do when they see he is rolling out.

■ *Roethlisberger is one of the NFL's toughest quarterbacks.*

Rooney, Art and Dan

In every way, Art Rooney, Sr., and his oldest son, Dan, have been vital parts of the NFL century.

Art founded the Pittsburgh Steelers' franchise in 1933, and then turned it over to his son in the late 1960s. Art continued to be involved from a distance, always with great admiration from fans and fellow owners, until his death in 1988 at age 87.

He was a tough act to follow for a son who was shyer, more sensitive, more re-served. And a little smarter, too. Art ran Steelers' teams that never finished first from 1933 though 1971. Dan built teams that were dominant forces in the game.

You didn't have to be powerful or rich to be Art's friend. "He always used to remind us that he wasn't a big shot and we weren't, either," Dan said. Dan and his four brothers, like their father, are men of the people.

Dan Rooney has been president and chairman of the Steelers for most of the past four decades. He also has been the team's unofficial director of human resources when it comes to firing (he has done that once, reluctantly) and hiring coaches (he has done that three times, carefully).

The firing was after the 1968 season. Bill Austin was released after three losing seasons. In 1969, Rooney hired Chuck Noll, who lasted 23 seasons and won four Super Bowls. In 1992, Rooney hired Bill Cowher, who lasted 15 seasons and won a Super Bowl. In 2007, Rooney hired Mike Tomlin, his third coach in 39 years. Over that same time period, the 31 other NFL teams made more than 325 coaching changes.

Art was part of the group that voted in commissioner Pete Rozelle in 1960. In 1989, Dan was pivotal in the election of Paul Tagliabue, who held the job for 17 years. Dan Rooney has played a large role in working with the players' association as well. Father and son are both in the Pro Football Hall of Fame. — J. W.

■ *Art Rooney was a beloved team owner.*

Rose Bowl

The Rose Bowl is a college football stadium located in Pasadena, California, near Los Angeles. The Rose Bowl has hosted the Super Bowl five times. The Super Bowl's five largest crowds have come in those games held at the beautiful stadium ringed by the San Gabriel Mountains.

The largest attendance was 103,985 for the Pittsburgh Steelers' 31-19 victory over the Los Angeles Rams in Super Bowl XIV in the 1979 season. In the other games at the Rose Bowl, the Raiders beat the Vikings 32-14 in Super Bowl XI (1976 season), the Redskins beat the Dolphins 27-17 in Super Bowl XVII (1982 season), the Giants beat the Broncos 39-20 in Super Bowl XXI (1986 season), and the Cowboys beat the Bills 52-17 in game XXVII (1992 season).

The annual Rose Bowl college football game has been played at the site each year since 1923 (except in 1942, when war-time travel restrictions forced the game to be played in Durham, North Carolina). The UCLA football team plays its home games at the Rose Bowl, as well. The Rose Bowl is also the site of top soccer games.

■ *Michael Vick rolls out, looking downfield for a target.*

Roughing

Roughing is a 15-yard, personal-foul penalty. Personal fouls can be called against any player, but roughing calls are for fouls against a kicker or a quarterback.

Roughing the kicker is called when a defensive player flagrantly runs into a kicker after the ball has been kicked. Similarly, roughing the quarterback is called when a defensive player obviously hits the quarterback after the ball has been thrown.

A referee indicates a roughing-the-kicker call by signaling a personal foul (on wrist

continued on page 51

Rozelle, Pete

It took three long days and 23 secret ballots for the 12 owners of National Football League teams to elect Pete Rozelle commissioner in late January 1960.

Rozelle was only 33 years old when he was chosen to succeed Bert Bell, who had died three months earlier. Rozelle was an unknown quantity, a man who had briefly held jobs with the Los Angeles Rams and in public relations.

The "unknown quantity" kept the commissioner's job for 29 years. He retired in 1989, the very model of what the head of a sport should be. Pete Rozelle seemed to have been born to be commissioner. He was a charming visionary who used the power of television to turn pro football into America's game.

In 1962, he negotiated the first national television contract—a then unprecedented $9.3 million pact with CBS. Today, TV contracts are worth billions.

The biggest challenge of the Rozelle era began in his first year on the job. The start-up American Football League was competition for the older league. Salary battles with the AFL escalated through the mid-1960s, but Rozelle worked behind the scenes to turn war into peace. The championship game between the two leagues became the biggest single event in sport—the Super Bowl. In 1970, the two leagues merged to form one 26-team league—under commissioner Pete Rozelle.

That same year, 1970, another brainchild of Rozelle's—Monday Night Football on ABC—was born. Pro football's bank accounts and audience both expanded.

In 1960, baseball clearly had been the national pastime. A decade later, pro football was the national passion. Rozelle's magic touch was the major reason, and the NFL has remained on top ever since.

Most of the highest-rated TV shows of all time are Super Bowls. The annual January spectacle was his favorite day. "I want people to leave the Super Bowl talking about everything they saw that day," said the man who died at 70 in 1996.

They did…and they still do. – J. W.

striking the other above his head), then swinging his leg; roughing the quarterback is the same, only with a raised arm.

Running Back

Running backs are the primary ball carriers—and often the biggest touchdown scorers—on a football team. Their number-one responsibility is to run the ball from scrimmage after taking a handoff or pitch (backward toss) from the quarterback. But they also are all-purpose offensive players who can be important short-range passing targets for a quarterback or key blockers in pass protection or for other runners.

Running backs come in all shapes and sizes. Halfbacks usually are smaller and quicker than fullbacks. Fullbacks are bigger and more effective as blockers or when short yardage is needed for a first down or a touchdown. Some backs are almost exclusively runners; others are better at catching the ball, and come into the game in passing situations. The very best running backs, such as San Diego superstar LaDainian Tomlinson, can perform all the duties of their position well, and stay on the field in almost any situation.

A standard offensive formation includes one fullback and one halfback (usually just called a run-

ning back). But some formations use two halfbacks for greater flexibility. Many teams also often utilize just one running back.

Rush

When a team runs on a play from scrimmage, the attempt is called a rush. But rush also can refer to the other side of the ball, when a defensive player or players tries to sack the quarterback or make him throw the ball sooner than he wants. This is known as a pass rush.

■ *Running back Larry Johnson heads upfield with the ball.*

Sack

When a defensive player tackles a quarterback who is attempting to pass, throwing him for a loss (or no gain), he is credited with a sack. Players who make the most sacks usually are the big money makers on defense.

Hall of Fame defensive end Deacon Jones, who played mostly for the Rams in a 14-year career that began in 1961, is credited for inventing the term "sack." He guessed that that short word would fit well in a newspaper headline.

Safety

The word "safety" can mean either a type of scoring play or a position in the defensive backfield.

Jevon Kearse (93) has just sacked QB Kyle Boller (7).

The safety that is a scoring play is usually recorded when a player in possession of the ball is tackled in his own end zone. These safeties also occur in other ways, such as when an offensive team is called for a penalty in its own end zone (for instance, holding) or when a punt is blocked out of the end zone. Teams that score a safety are awarded two points. The referee signals a safety by playing both hands above his head with palms touching. After a safety, the team that earned the points receives a free kick that originates at the opposing team's 20-yard line.

A safety also is one of the positions, along with a cornerback, that plays in the defensive backfield, which also can be called the secondary. The standard defense most teams play features a strong safety and a free safety. The strong safety lines up on the same side of the field as the offensive team's tight end; the free safety can roam where needed and help other players in pass defense.

Each safety must be a sure tackler, though. That's because a safety is a team's last line of defense. A wide receiver who beats a cornerback guarding him often has only the safety between him and the end zone.

Sanders, Barry

Barry Sanders was an electrifying runner with a vast assortment of eye-popping moves that often left defensive players grasping at air. Sanders could stop, start, cut back, make a spin move, and reverse direction in the blink of an eye—and sometimes all on one play. He played 10 seasons for the Detroit Lions from 1989 to 1998, then stunned the NFL world by retiring before the 1999 season. Sanders still was among the league's best players when he decided to walk away. Not since the legendary Jim Brown in 1965 had any NFL running back retired while still so productive.

Only two years earlier, in 1997, Sanders became just the third NFL player to run for more than 2,000 yards in a season, gaining 2,053. In his final season, he ran for 1,491 yards, marking his 10th consecutive 1,000-yard season. In all, he gained 15,269 yards on the ground. Only Emmitt Smith (18,355) and Walter Payton (16,726) ever had more. Sanders also ran for 99 touchdowns and scored 109 total touchdowns in his career, figures that ranked among the NFL's all-time top 10 at the time of his retirement.

■ *Sanders was an eye-popping running back.*

A former Heisman Trophy winner at Oklahoma State, Sanders was inducted into the Pro Football Hall of Fame in his first year of eligibility in 2004.

The Rams celebrate their 1955 Western Division title.

St. Louis Rams

The Rams have played in the NFL since 1937. Win or lose, good teams or bad (and it's mostly been good), they always seem to be among the most entertaining and high-scoring clubs in the league.

The franchise began as the Cleveland Rams in 1937. The Rams won one NFL championship in Cleveland—in 1945, their final year there—before moving to Los Angeles in 1946. The Los Angeles Rams were NFL champions in 1951 and built a large and loyal following there. The highlight was a spot in Super Bowl XIV, where they fell to the Steelers. But in 1995, the team moved to St. Louis. In their fifth year in their new town, the Rams won the Super Bowl for the first time, beating Tennessee 23-16 in game XXXIV.

Dating all the way to their years in Cleveland, the Rams' offenses have featured some of the superstars in the NFL. In 1945, for instance, quarterback Bob Waterfield joined the club. He had a sensational rookie season, passing for 1,609 yards and 14 touchdowns, and leading the Rams to 9 victories in 10 games. Waterfield was named the league's most valuable player, and capped the year by quarterbacking the team to a 15-14 victory over the Washington Redskins in the NFL Championship Game.

Waterfield was young, athletic, and handsome. Los Angeles embraced its new star when the team moved to California the next year. Waterfield even married a movie star, actress Jane Russell. But there soon was another famous quarterback on the Rams' roster named Norm Van Brocklin. He and Waterfield shared quarterbacking duties for the 1951 Rams, who won the league title.

Waterfield, Van Brocklin, Tom Fears, as well as end Elroy "Crazylegs" Hirsch, all eventually made it to the Pro Football Hall of Fame. They gave the Rams some of the most-well-known players in the league in the early 1950s. They also gave the Rams the

NFL's most powerful offense. The 1950 squad scored 466 points in only 12 games. Their average of 38.3 points per game is the highest in league history.

The 1999 Rams were one of the few teams in NFL history with an offense nearly as explosive as the 1950 squad's. Dick Vermeil was head coach in '99, and Mike Martz, who would become the head coach the next year, was the offensive coordinator. Kurt Warner came from out of nowhere in the Arena League to become the pass-happy quarterback. Marshall Faulk was a running back who could catch the ball as well as run it. And Isaac Bruce and Torry Holt gave the Rams a great set of wide receivers. The Rams' teams of the late 1990s and early 2000s were dubbed "The Greatest Show on Turf."

That group put on a show, all right, scoring 526 points (the third-most in a season in NFL history) en route to winning the Super Bowl. The next year, the Rams scored 540 points, making them the only team ever to crack the 500-point mark in back-to-back years.

Despite all the fireworks on offense, the Rams have featured some excellent play-ers on the defensive side of the ball, too. The "Fearsome Foursome" defensive line was famous during the 1960s and early 1970s. Future Pro Football Hall of Fame members Merlin Olsen and Deacon Jones keyed that line.

■ *Isaac Bruce remains a key target for Rams' QBs.*

Another future Hall of Famer, defensive end Jack Youngblood, helped the team win an NFL-record seven consecutive division championships from 1973 to 1979. The Rams could not, however, win a Super Bowl in that span. (The AFC's Pittsburgh Steelers won four of them in those years.)

The current Rams are trying to carve their own identity under coach Scott Linehan, who took over in 2006. Not surprisingly, though, Linehan's first team had several stars on offense. Quarterback Marc Bulger, wide receiver Torry Holt, and running back Steven Jackson all made the Pro Bowl, the NFL's annual all-star game played in Hawaii.

ST. LOUIS RAMS

CONFERENCE: NFC

DIVISION: WEST

TEAM COLORS:
GOLD, BLUE, AND WHITE

STADIUM (CAPACITY):
EDWARD JONES DOME
(66,000)

ALL-TIME RECORD:
(THROUGH 2006):
517–465–20

NFL CHAMPIONSHIPS
(MOST RECENT):
3 (1999)

San Diego Chargers

The Chargers were one of the original AFL franchises in 1960. Over the years, the club has had many successful teams—including a league champion in 1963 and a Super Bowl participant in 1994—and excellent and colorful players. But for San Diego fans, there's no time quite like the present. The team won more games in the 2006 season than ever before. And it features one of football's biggest superstars.

The San Diego Chargers actually began their existence as the Los Angeles Chargers in 1960. They played their home games in the AFL's inaugural season in the Los Angeles Memorial Coliseum before heading a short drive south in time for the 1961 season.

The Chargers were successful right from the start. They were the AFL Western Conference champs in 1960 before losing to the Houston Oilers in the league championship game. They made it to the title match tin 1961, too, only to lose to Houston again.

Quarterback Jack Kemp, a future U.S. Congressman, was the Chargers' first star. He led the club in passing in 1960 and 1961. But the Chargers lost him to Buffalo during the 1962 season. Kemp eventually led the Bills to AFL Championship Game victories in 1964 and 1965 against—as you might have guessed—the Chargers.

In between all those championship-game losses, San Diego did win its lone title in 1963. Former NFL star Tobin Rote was the quarterback, and the Chargers' strong offense featured a 1,000-yard rusher in Paul Lowe (1,010 yards) and a 1,000-yard pass

■ *Strong-armed Dan Fouts led "Air Coryell."*

catcher in future Hall of Famer Lance Alworth (1,205 yards). In their 51-10 championship game win over Boston, running back Keith Lincoln amassed 349 total yards and scored two touchdowns.

The Chargers played most of their AFL existence under future Hall of Fame coach Sid Gillman. They posted a winning record nine times in the league's 10 seasons. But their transition to the NFL beginning in 1970 was not as smooth. They had a series of losing years before offensive mastermind Don Coryell took over as coach in 1978.

The "Air Coryell" offense turned the Chargers into winners again. Though they couldn't quite make it to the Super Bowl, the Chargers were one of the league's most exciting teams. Quarterback Dan Fouts, tight end Kellen Winslow, and wide receiver Charlie Joiner all made it to the Hall of Fame.

In 1994, the Chargers reached the Super Bowl for the first time under coach Bobby Ross. But San Francisco was too strong, and won game XXIX, 49-26.

In 2001, current star LaDainian Tomlinson arrived as a first-round draft choice out of Texas Christian. As a rookie, he rushed for 1,236 yards and scored 10 touchdowns. And in his first five seasons, he averaged 1,472 yards rushing and 16 touchdowns per year. But not even those incredible statistics prepared anyone for what happened in 2006.

■ *Tomlinson's 186 points in 2006 set an all-time record.*

That year, Tomlinson turned in the greatest single season by a running back in NFL history. He ran for 1,815 yards, gained 2,323 yards from scrimmage (rushing and receiving), and scored a record 31 touchdowns. He even passed for two touchdowns!

More importantly, Tomlinson's amazing performance helped the Chargers post the NFL's best record at 14-2. Although head coach Marty Schottenheimer's team was upset by the Patriots in the divisional playoffs, San Diego fans can't wait to see what's in store for the team in 2007—and beyond.

SAN DIEGO CHARGERS

CONFERENCE: AFC

DIVISION: WEST

TEAM COLORS:
NAVY BLUE, WHITE, AND GOLD

STADIUM (CAPACITY):
QUALCOMM STADIUM (70,000)

ALL-TIME RECORD:
(THROUGH 2006):
350–367–11

NFL CHAMPIONSHIPS (MOST RECENT, INCLUDES AFL):
11 (1963)

San Francisco 49ers

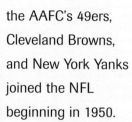

After several decades of frustration, San Francisco emerged as the NFL's dominant team of the 1980s. The '90s were good, too, giving the 49ers one of the longest periods of success in league history.

San Francisco began its existence in the All-America Football Conference (AAFC) in 1946. That league went out of business after only four seasons, but the AAFC's 49ers, Cleveland Browns, and New York Yanks joined the NFL beginning in 1950.

Though the 49ers fielded many high-scoring and successful teams in their first 35 years, they couldn't quite win a championship. In their AAFC years, for instance, they were the league's second-best team—but the Browns won the title

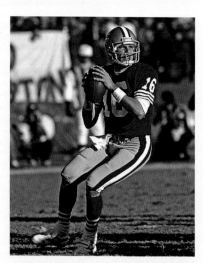

■ *Montana was a 49ers legend.*

each season. In the NFL in 1957, they lost a Western Conference playoff to eventual league champ Detroit after leading 27-7 in the third quarter. Then, in the early 1970s, they won three consecutive NFC West titles. Each year, though, the Dallas Cowboys ended the 49ers' Super Bowl hopes.

It looked as if 1981 might turn out the same way, too. The 49ers were the surprise team of the regular season, winning 13 games in Bill Walsh's third season as coach, but found themselves trailing the Cowboys 27-21 late in the fourth quarter of the NFC Championship Game. Quarterback Joe Montana, though, led the 49ers on one of the most memorable drives in NFL history. San Francisco marched 89 yards to a touchdown, taking a 28-27 lead with 51 seconds to play on Montana's scoring pass to leaping wide receiver Dwight Clark. "The Catch," as the play is known, put the 49ers in the Super Bowl (game XVI) for the first time.

San Francisco won that Super Bowl, beating the Cincinnati Bengals 26-21, but the 49ers were just warming up. Before the 1980s were over, they added three more Super

SAN FRANCISCO 49ERS

CONFERENCE: NFC

DIVISION: WEST

TEAM COLORS: METALLIC GOLD, CARDINAL RED, AND BEIGE

STADIUM (CAPACITY): MONSTER PARK (69,732)

ALL-TIME RECORD: (THROUGH 2006): 470–385–13

NFL CHAMPIONSHIPS (MOST RECENT): 5 (1994)

Bowl championships. Montana was named the most valuable player in three of the four Super Bowl victories, and Jerry Rice was the MVP in the other. Rice, a first-round draft pick in 1985, the year after San Francisco beat the Dolphins in Super Bowl XIX, would go on to become the most successful wide receiver in NFL history. He was the MVP of Super Bowl XXIII, when he had 215 receiving yards in a 20-16 victory over the Bengals. Montana's winning TD pass in the final minute, however, was caught by John Taylor.

Walsh retired after that game and turned the coaching reins over to George Seifert, his defensive coordinator. Seifert directed the club to its fourth Super Bowl title in 1989 (a 55-10 rout of the Broncos in game XXIV), plus another championship in 1994 (a 49-26 victory over the Chargers in Super Bowl XXIX). The latter title was the first with Steve Young at quarterback. Young passed for a record six touchdowns in the game, including three to Rice, and was the game's MVP.

In all, the 49ers won five Super Bowls in the 14 seasons from 1981 to 1994. They posted 16 consecutive winning seasons from 1983 to 1998. Walsh, Montana, Young, and defensive back Ronnie Lott are 49ers from that era who already have been inducted into the Pro Football Hall of Fame. Rice is sure to join them when he becomes eligible in 2010.

Rice was awesome, but it is great quarterbacks that have been the Niners' hallmark. In addition to Montana and Young, two of best ever, the 49ers' legacy includes other star signal callers such as Frankie Albert, Y.A. Tittle, John Brodie, and Jeff Garcia. The club hopes that it found its next great quarterback in Alex Smith, who was the top overall pick of the 2005 draft. Smith and young running back Frank Gore helped make coach Mike Nolan's team a surprise playoff contender in 2006.

■ *Frank Gore is a power runner for the 49ers.*

■ *Warren Sapp takes up a lot of room.*

Safety Blitz

A type of blitz in which a safety abandons his pass-coverage duties to chase the quarterback at the snap of the ball. A blitz is when a defense rushes more than just defensive linemen at the QB.

It is a risky play because the defense leaves itself without a key component of its pass coverage. But the reward for surprising the offense with such a maneuver can be a game-changing sack or a turnover.

St. Louis Rams

Please see page 54.

Salary Cap

The salary cap is a specific dollar amount that each NFL team can spend on player contracts for its entire roster. This is to maintain balance among teams. It prevents the teams with the most money and richest owners from signing all of the best players. With a few exceptions, no team can spend more than the "cap number" each year.

There are many different rules governing the salary cap. They can be so complicated that most NFL teams employ a specific person (sometimes called a "capologist") strictly to deal with this facet of a club's operation.

San Diego Chargers

Please see page 56.

San Francisco 49ers

Please see page 58.

Sapp, Warren

Warren Sapp is an all-star defensive tackle who played for the Oakland Raiders in the 2006 season. His best years came while playing for the Tampa Bay Buccaneers from 1995 to 2003. In 2004, he signed with Oakland as a free agent. At 6 feet 2 and 300 pounds, but with the quickness of a smaller man, Sapp is a powerful force against the run. What really sets him apart, however, is his ability to rush the passer as well. Most of the NFL's top pass rushers play defensive end or outside linebacker. Sapp provides an added dimension to the defense by creating pressure from the interior of the defensive line. His

94.5 career sacks are among the most by an interior lineman in NFL history.

Sapp has had 10 or more sacks in a season four times, with a career best of 16.5 in 2000. He was playing for Tampa Bay at the time. The Buccaneers chose him in the first round of the '95 draft out of Miami, and he was in the starting lineup on Kickoff Week-

Sayers, Gale

Gale Sayers was a dazzling running back and kick returner for the Chicago Bears from 1965 to 1971. Despite such a short career, he was inducted into the Pro Football Hall of Fame in his first year of eligibility in 1977.

Sayers' rise to stardom was meteoric, though his nickname was for a different celestial body: The Wichita native and former Kansas University standout was called the "Kansas Comet." He burst onto the scene as a rookie in 1965 when he scored 22 touchdowns. That's still the NFL single-season mark for a first-year player. Six of his scores came in one game against the San Francisco 49ers. He was only the third player in league history to reach the end zone six times in one game; no one has done it since.

His breakaway speed combined with shifty moves made Sayers a threat to score a touchdown every time he touched the ball. In his career, he scored 39 touchdowns rushing,

nine receiving, six on kickoff returns, and two on punt returns. Unfortunately, knee injuries eventually took their toll and forced his early retirement. When he was inducted into the Hall of Fame at 34 years old, he was the youngest member of the shrine.

■ *Sayers's greatness shined for a short time.*

end of his rookie season. Two years later, he made the Pro Bowl for the first of seven consecutive seasons. In 2002, he played a key role as Tampa Bay won the Super Bowl for the first time in franchise history.

Scramble

 A scramble is the action of a quarterback who has dropped back to pass and is trying to avoid being sacked by the defense behind the line of scrimmage.

A quarterback with the ability to scramble effectively can be a potent weapon for an offense. Historically, some of the great scramblers include Pro Football Hall of Famers such as John Elway, Fran Tarkenton, Roger Staubach, and Steve Young. Currently, Tony Romo and Michael Vick

Schmidt, Joe

■ *Ultra-tough Schmidt won two NFL titles.*

Joe Schmidt, a member of the Hall of Fame's Class of 1973, was one of the NFL's first great middle linebackers in the 1950s. He was the leader of the Lions' proud defense in a 13-year career from 1953 to 1965.

Schmidt was not the league's first middle linebacker (the Bears' Bill George usually is credited with being that), but he was one of the best. He made the Pro Bowl 10 consecutive years beginning in 1955. He was a smart player who endlessly studied his opponents and knew what plays to anticipate. One measure of the respect his teammates had for him is that they voted Schmidt their captain nine times, and their MVP four times.

When Schmidt joined the Lions as a seventh-round draft pick in 1953, Detroit was coming off a league championship the previous season. He helped the club repeat as champions in his rookie year, then win another title in 1957.

Schramm, Tex

The man who built the Dallas Cowboys from scratch and was their president and general manager for 30 years was named Texas . . . but was born in California.

However, Tex Schramm graduated from the University of Texas in 1947 and returned to Texas to stay in 1960. His genius helped guide the Cowboys to the top of the NFL world, where they became America's Team.

Schramm's first job out of college was working in publicity for the Los Angeles Rams, later rising to general manager. After a stint with CBS Sports, he was hired in 1960 by Cowboys owner Clint Murchison to put together his new expansion team. Schramm began by hiring Tom Landry as coach. The Cowboys started slowly, finishing 0-11-1 in 1960, but things turned around soon. Once they did, there was no looking back for one of the most successful franchises in all of sports.

The Cowboys had 20 consecutive winning seasons beginning in 1996, the third-longest winning streak in sports history. They won 13 division titles, played in five Super Bowls, and won Super Bowls VI and XII.

In 1966, Schramm was a key figure in negotiations between the NFL and the American Football League, which led to the merger in 1970, and created the championship game

■ *Schramm was the man behind the Cowboys.*

that became known as the Super Bowl. The first Super Bowl was played in 1967.

Schramm also was known for his innovations that helped redefine the modern NFL. The Dallas Cowboys Cheerleaders were his idea. He advanced computer technology in scouting, and championed instant replay. Throughout his time with Dallas, he always looked for new ways to improve the team.

Schramm received the NFL's Bert Bell Award for outstanding executive leadership in 1978. He was inducted into the Pro Football Hall of Fame in 1991. A few months after he died in 2003 (at 83), he was inducted into the Cowboys' Ring of Honor. — J. W.

rank among the game's top scramblers (although Vick may be characterized more as a straight runner than a scrambler).

Screen Pass

A short pass—forward but behind the line of scrimmage—to a player, usually a running back, who has two or more offensive linemen blocking in front of him (forming a "screen"). Usually, the pass is to

■ *Seau is one of the NFL's fiercest tacklers.*

one side of the field or the other, although "middle screens" have become popular in recent years, too.

A screen pass is a particularly effective method of slowing down a pass rush. The offensive linemen let the pass rushers go by them, then force the defenders to reverse field and chase the pass catcher.

The screen pass first was introduced to the NFL by Redskins coach Ray Flaherty. He used it to great effect in Washington's victory over the Bears in the 1937 league title game.

Seau, Junior

As sure as a first down is 10 yards or a quarter is 15 minutes, Junior Seau headed to Hawaii every year as a linebacker on the AFC Pro Bowl squad in the 1990s. Almost every year, anyway. Seau entered the NFL when the Chargers selected him out of Southern California with the fifth overall pick of the 1990 draft. By the next season, he earned his first all-star selection—and the first of 12 in a row (although he missed the 2002 game because of injury). He was a member of the NFL's 1990's All-Decade Team.

An athletic linebacker with a reputation for inspired, emotional play, Seau can defend the run well or drop into pass coverage. After playing 13 seasons with the Chargers, he signed with Miami in 2003. He briefly retired in 2006, but reconsid-

■ *A hard-working Art Shell takes a breather.*

Shell, Art

Art Shell had a significant impact on the NFL not only on the playing field, but also on the sidelines. Shell was first a Hall of Fame tackle for the Raiders from 1968 to 1982, and later became the first African-American head coach in more than 60 years when he took over the reins of the Raiders in 1989.

Shell played in 207 regular-season games for the Raiders and earned eight Pro Bowl selections. He is best remembered for a near-flawless performance while playing opposite Vikings defensive end Jim Marshall in Super Bowl XI in the 1976 season. Marshall wasn't in on a single tackle, and Oakland won, 32-14. Shell later helped the Raiders win Super Bowl XV in the 1980 season.

Four games into the 1989 season, Shell succeeded Mike Shanahan as the Raiders' head coach. He was the first African-American to lead an NFL team since Fritz Pollard in the 1920s. Shell turned the Raiders' fortunes around, taking them to the brink of the playoffs that year. The next season, they reached the AFC Championship Game. Shell coached through 1994. He also had an unsuccessful one-season return as the club's coach in 2006.

ered and joined the New England Patriots instead for one season.

Seau's given first name is Tiaina. He was born in San Diego, but spent much of his childhood in American Samoa. His last name is pronounced "SAY-ow."

Secondary

Another name for the defensive backfield. The secondary is composed of the cornerbacks and safeties. A standard defense has two of each. The secondary

continued on page 68

Seattle Seahawks

The Seattle Seahawks originally entered the NFL as an expansion franchise in 1976. They made big strides in their early years. Now, in recent seasons, they have taken the next step up to become one of the league's elite teams.

■ *Largent wasn't fast . . . he was just great.*

Seattle joined the NFL the same season as fellow expansion team Tampa Bay. The Seahawks played their first season as a member of the NFC West, with the understanding that they would shift to the AFC West the following season. They remained in the AFC until the league's latest realignment plan in 2002 shifted them back to the NFC West.

The initial Seattle team was surprisingly competitive under coach Jack Patera. The Seahawks nearly beat St. Louis in the first game in their franchise history, losing 30-24 when the Cardinals intercepted a pass in the end zone on the final play. Still, Seattle won only two games that year, including one against the Buccaneers in what was called the "Expansion Bowl."

By 1978, though, the Seahawks were winners. Their 9-7 record that year was, at the time, the best ever by a third-year expansion team. They built that mark with one of the best offenses in the league. Jim Zorn was an exciting, left-handed quarterback who also could scramble effectively. Future Hall of Fame wide receiver Steve Largent blossomed into one of the best pass catchers in the league. He had 71 receptions for 1,168 yards and eight touchdowns while making the Pro Bowl for the first of seven times in his career.

Largent helped Seattle score more points than all but six other NFL teams did that year. Unfortunately, the early Seahawks' defenses could not match up to the club's strong offenses.

That started to change when Chuck Knox was hired as coach in 1983. In the 1970s, Knox had made the Los Angeles Rams a division champion. And in his first year in Seattle, the Seahawks rose to the top of the AFC West, going 9-7. They even won the first two postseason games in their franchise history before the Oakland Raiders ended Seattle's Super Bowl hopes in the AFC title game.

The same year that Knox arrived, so did rookie running back Curt Warner. He rushed for 1,449 yards as a rookie to give Seattle the biggest rushing threat in its brief history. Warner would go on to play seven years for the Seahawks (although he missed almost all of 1984 after being injured in the first game). By the time he left the club following the 1989 season, he was the franchise's all-time leading rusher with 6,705 yards.

Chris Warren came along in the 1990s and broke Warner's mark (by just one yard), just as quarterback Dave Krieg eventually broke Zorn's career passing records. Now, in the 2000s, the Seahawks feature two more of the club's all-time greats in

quarterback Matt Hasselbeck and running back Shaun Alexander. Those players helped the Seahawks, under coach Mike Holmgren, reach the Super Bowl for the first time in the 2005 season. Seattle lost that game to Pittsburgh, but a third consecutive NFC West title in '06 has Seahawks' fans excited about the future.

■ *RB Shaun Alexander leads the way for Seattle today.*

Throughout the franchise history, those fans have remained among the most vocal and supportive in the entire league. In fact, in 1984, the club retired uniform number 12—not for any player, but because the crowd represents the Seahawks' "12th Man." The Seattle crowds used to make a deafening roar in home games played at the Kingdome. The Seahawks don't play indoors anymore (they moved into new Qwest Field in 2002), but the fans are just as noisy, giving the club a definite home-field advantage.

SEATTLE SEAHAWKS

CONFERENCE: NFC

DIVISION: WEST

TEAM COLORS: BLUE, NAVY, AND BRIGHT GREEN

STADIUM (CAPACITY): QWEST FIELD (67,000)

ALL-TIME RECORD: (THROUGH 2006): 242–257–0

NFL CHAMPIONSHIPS (MOST RECENT): NONE

also includes any extra defensive backs brought into the game for added pass protection (sometimes called "nickel backs" or "dime backs").

Shea Stadium

Shea Stadium was the home of the New York Jets from the time it opened in 1964 through the 1983 season. The Giants also played there in 1975 while awaiting completion of Giants Stadium in East Rutherford, New Jersey. (Both clubs now play at Giants Stadium.)

The stadium was the site of the Jets' thrilling, 27-23 victory over Oakland in the 1968 AFL title game. The win sent them to the lone Super Bowl in their franchise history. Quarterback Joe Namath passed for three touchdowns in that game, including the game-winner in the fourth quarter, despite icy winds. Cold and wind were common in late-season games at Shea.

The multipurpose stadium was the first that could be converted from a baseball site to a football site by motorized stands that rolled back and forth. Shea has served as the home of baseball's New York Mets since 1964. The Yankees played there, too, while Yankee Stadium was being renovated in the mid-1970s. The famous English rock group The Beatles played several sold-out concerts there. Pope John Paul II said Mass at Shea as well.

Shockey, Jeremy

Jeremy Shockey is an all-star tight end for the New York Giants. He made the Pro Bowl for the fourth time in his first five NFL seasons in 2006.

A first-round draft pick out of Miami in 2002, Shockey was the 14th overall pick that year. Through 2006, he had averaged 63 catches for 722 yards and 5 touchdowns per season in his career—excellent pass-catching numbers for an NFL tight end.

Unfortunately, Shockey often has made as many headlines off the field as on it. He has angered opposing coaches and players, as well as his own coaches and teammates, with his sometimes-brash comments.

Shoes

The football shoes that a player wears depends on the type of surface on which he is playing, as well as the condition of the field. For games on artificial turf, a player wears rubber-soled shoes that give him better traction. For games on natural grass, he wears shoes with cleats. When the field is dry and footing is sure, he'll have short cleats to run faster. When the field is wet or muddy, he'll have longer cleats to dig into the ground. Equipment men can change the length of a player's cleats during a game. The cleats are usually interchangeable. Most players also have layers of tape wrapped around their shoe and ankle to provide additional support.

Shotgun Formation

In a conventional offensive formation, the quarterback takes the snap directly from the center. But in the Shotgun formation, he stands three to five yards behind the center and catches a long snap. This gives the quarterback the advantage of surveying the entire field right away at the snap. But it also tips off the defense that a pass is likely coming.

San Francisco coach Red Hickey started the Shotgun in 1960, and it was an immediate success. But as opposing teams caught on in 1961, he scrapped the system. The Dallas Cowboys eventually instituted their own version of the Shotgun in the 1970s, and many NFL teams now employ it in passing situations.

Shoulder Pads

Along with the helmet, the shoulder pads are the most unique, and important, pieces of a football player's equipment. They help absorb the shock of physical contact in order to prevent injury. Modern shoulder pads have an air-impact system that makes them smaller and lighter than ever before. At the same time, they are even safer for the players.

Players at different positions wear different size shoulder pads. For instance, quarterbacks, whose arm motion can't be restricted, wear smaller pads than linebackers or offensive linemen, who are in collisions on almost every play.

Shoulder pads are just part of a wide array of pads that a player can use. Other pads include thigh pads, knee pads, elbow pads, hip pads, rib pads, and more.

Shovel Pass

A shovel pass is a short pass forward, usually to a running back just a yard or two in front of the quarterback. It is sometimes made by design from the Shotgun formation. A quarterback essentially pushes the ball forward on a shovel pass.

Linebackers like Brian Urlacher wear very large shoulder pads.

A shovel pass is almost like a long handoff. But because the ball is flipped forward, it is a pass. If it is mishandled or falls to the ground untouched, it is incomplete.

Sideline

The sideline is the collective area where coaches, players who are not on the field for a particular play, and trainers and other personnel are gathered.

The sideline also refers to the actual white line that marks the boundary of the long sides of the field. The sideline is considered out of bounds. If a player in posses-sion of the ball touches any part of the line, the play is over.

Signals

When a quarterback reaches the line of scrimmage before the start of a play, he communicates to his teammates through a series of signals. They are usually voiced signals but occasionally, especially in noisy environments, can be hand signals, too.

Signals can be in code words or numbers. They are used to set the offense and prepare for the snap. They also can be used

Players such as Indianapolis' Peyton Manning (18) meet with coaches on the sideline during a game.

Shula, Don

Was Don Shula the greatest coach in the history of the National Football League? It is difficult to examine his numbers and say otherwise.

Shula won 347 games in 33 seasons as an NFL coach (seven in Baltimore, 1963-69, and 26 in Miami, 1970-1995). He won 23 more games than the second winningest coach, George Halas, did in 40 years (324). Shula also owns the NFL's only perfect season, guiding the 1972 Dolphins to a 17-0 record, a feat not matched before or since.

Shula's Dolphins won back-to-back Super Bowls, winning Super Bowl VII 14-7 over Washington and Super Bowl VIII over Minnesota 24-7. His teams played in four other Super Bowls. He retired after the 1995 season, and in 1997, to no one's surprise, was swept into the Pro Football Hall of Fame.

It was an amazing career for a player originally drafted in the ninth round by the Cleveland Browns in 1951. He had a seven-year playing career with three teams before deciding to become a coach. After working in the college ranks, he returned to pro football in 1960 to the Detroit Lions as a defensive assistant. In 1963, he was named to succeed Weeb Ewbank as the head coach of the Baltimore Colts. At 33, he was the youngest head coach in NFL history.

■ *Best ever? Well, he won the most games.*

Under Shula, the Colts had seven consecutive winning seasons. The team reached the NFL title game in 1964 and 1968.

In 1970, Shula left Baltimore to become the head coach of the Miami Dolphins, a fifth-year expansion team that had won just three games the previous season. Shula's first two Miami teams made the playoffs, setting the stage for the perfect 1972 season.

Shula's Dolphins returned to the Super Bowl after the 1982 and 1984 seasons but those visits ended in frustration.

On November 14, 1993, Shula passed Halas to become the most successful coach in NFL history when he registered victory No. 325. — J. W.

to change a play at the line of scrimmage (see "Audible") or pick from an option of two plays in the huddle. Or they can mean virtually nothing. Sometimes they are used just to confuse the opposition. At the same time, the center may be calling signals to communicate blocking assignments on the offensive line, while a linebacker is calling signals for the defense.

Signals also can refer to the actions of the referee while assessing a penalty. He uses hand signals to indicate the type of foul and which team is penalized to the sidelines, crowd, and media (although referees also have wireless microphones that also allow them to voice such information).

Singletary, Mike

Linebacker Mike Singletary was the heart and soul of the Bears' defense for 12 seasons beginning in 1981. In 1998, he was inducted into the Hall of Fame.

■ *Sadly, Simpson is now infamous.*

Simpson, O.J.

O.J. Simpson was the NFL's first 2,000-yard rusher. He gained 2,003 yards while playing for the Buffalo Bills in 1973. That was one of four league rushing titles that he won in his 11-year NFL career with the Bills (1969-1977) and 49ers (1978-79). In all, he rushed for 11,236 yards. In 1985, he was inducted into the Pro Football Hall of Fame in his first year of eligibility.

Simpson's name, however, will forever be linked to the murders of his ex-wife and another man in June of 1994. He was arrested and put on trial for those murders. Simpson was acquitted of the criminal charges in court, but later was found liable for the deaths by a civil court. (A civil court cannot send anyone to jail, but can force the defendant to pay monetary damages.)

Smith, Bruce

Former defensive end Bruce Smith is the NFL's all-time leader with an even 200 sacks in a 19-year career that ended in 2003.

Buffalo chose Smith with the number-one overall pick in the 1985 draft out of Virginia Tech, and he went on to play 15 seasons with the Bills. He played his last four seasons (2000-03) with the Washington Redskins. He posted five sacks in his final season at age 40 to break Reggie White's previous league record of 198 career sacks.

Though Smith never led the league in sacks, he had 10 or more sacks an incredible 14 times in his 19 NFL seasons. He had a career-best 19 sacks in 1990, when he earned the first of his two Associated Press NFL defensive player of the year awards (the other was in 1996) and helped the Bills reach the Super Bowl for the first time. Buffalo lost a narrow, 20-19 decision to the Giants in game XXV that year despite a safety that Smith recorded when he sacked New York quarterback Jeff Hostetler in the end zone. (Buffalo returned to the Super Bowl each of the next three years, too, but failed to win each time.) Smith earned 11 Pro Bowl selections in his career. He will be eligible for induction into the Pro Football Hall of Fame in 2009.

■ *Bruce Smith was a sack artist.*

Almost anyone who watched Singletary play was struck by the intensity and focus that he brought to the middle linebacker position. He was the anchor of the Bears' "46" defense that overwhelmed opponents during the mid-1980s. In Chicago's Super Bowl-winning season of 1985, Singletary was named the Associated Press' NFL defensive player of the year. He earned the same honor three years later. He also earned 10 Pro Bowl selections, and is considered among the best ever.

■ *Smith is No. 1 all-time in rushing.*

Smith, Emmitt

Emmitt Smith is the NFL's all-time leading rusher. He gained 18,355 yards in a 15-year NFL career, mostly with the Dallas Cowboys, from 1990 to 2004.

A first-round draft pick out of Florida in 1990, Smith made an immediate impact in the NFL. He ran for 937 yards and 11 touchdowns as a rookie to help Dallas improve from a woeful 1-15 record the year before he arrived to 7-9. By the next season, the Cowboys were in the playoffs, and Smith cracked the 1,000-yard rushing mark (1,563) for the first of 11 consecutive seasons.

Beginning in 1992, Dallas won three Super Bowls in a four-year span. Smith was named the MVP of the Cowboys' 30-13 victory over Buffalo in game XXVIII after he rushed for 132 yards and two second-half touchdowns. That capped a 1993 season in which he also won his third consecutive NFL rushing title (1,486 yards) and earned league MVP honors. The eight-time Pro Bowl selection is likely a first-ballot Hall of Famer when he becomes eligible in 2010.

Smith has remained competitive in his post-playing career. He is frequently seen at celebrity golf tournaments, and in 2006 he won television's *Dancing With the Stars* competition along with partner Cheryl Burke, a professional dancer.

Since his playing career ended, Singletary has become an NFL assistant coach. In 2005, he became the assistant head coach of the San Francisco 49ers. Singletary's name often is included among the candidates for vacant NFL head-coaching positions.

"Sixty-Minute Men"

The Sixty-Minute Men were players from a different era. They played offense, defense, and, often, special teams, too (thus the entire 60 minutes of a game).

Sixty-Minute Men, or "two-way players," were common in the first few decades of the NFL (the 1920s through the 1940s), when rosters were smaller in number and rules limited free substitution. As those rules loosened, and as players began to specialize on offense, defense, or the kicking game, the Sixty-Minute Men became a dying breed in the 1950s.

Pro Football Hall of Famer Chuck Bednarik (1949-1962) is considered the last of the Sixty-Minute Men. Bednarik played center on offense and tackle on defense. He played both ways throughout the Eagles' 17-13 victory over Green Bay in the 1960 NFL Championship Game. He secured Philadelphia's win with a touchdown-saving tackle on the final play.

Smith, Steve

Carolina Panthers wide receiver Steve Smith is one of the top breakaway pass-catching threats in the NFL today. Despite missing the first two games in 2006, he amassed 1,166 yards on 83 catches and made the Pro Bowl for the third time in his six-year career (including once as a kick returner).

Smith's '06 performance came on the heels of a league-leading 1,563-yard season (on 103 receptions) in 2005. Many of those yards came after the catch; many NFL observers believe Smith is best wide receiver in the league after he grabs the ball.

Smith shared the NFL comeback player of the year award for 2005 along with Patriots linebacker Tedy Bruschi. Smith had missed almost the entire 2004 season after breaking his leg on Kickoff Weekend that year.

■ *Not that big, but oh so fast: Steve Smith on the go.*

■ *Football's most famous tractor: Thanks to this driver, the Patriots booted a game-winning field goal.*

Snap

The snap is the exchange of the ball from the center (almost always to the quarterback) at the beginning of every play from scrimmage. It is a basic skill that must be mastered. A poor snap can ruin a play from the start.

On regular plays from scrimmage, the center hands the ball right into the quarterback's hands or snaps it a short way back in the Shotgun formation. On kicking plays, the snap can go from 7 to 15 yards back to a holder or punter. A player called a long snapper handles the snap on special-teams plays.

"Sneakers Game"

The New York Giants beat the Chicago Bears 30-13 in the 1934 NFL Championship Game in what has come to be known as the "Sneakers Game." That's because the Giants donned basketball shoes while trailing in the second half to gain better footing on the icy field in New York.

End Ray Flaherty, who had played college football on icy fields in the Pacific Northwest, pitched the idea of wearing sneakers to Giants coach Steve Owen before the game. So an equipment man was dispatched to find some shoes. It was Sunday, though, and all the sporting goods stores in New York were closed! By the time he found some sneakers to borrow from a nearby college, the Giants trailed 10-3 at halftime.

New York soon fell further behind, at 13-3. But with their players getting better traction because of their sneakers, the Giants scored 27 consecutive points in the fourth quarter to win one of the most famous games in NFL history.

"Snow-Plow Game"

The New England Patriots beat the division-rival Miami Dolphins 3-0 in the "Snow-Plow Game" in December of 1982.

The game got its nickname because the only points came when a snow-plow operator drove his tractor onto the field and cleared a patch of turf for New England's John Smith to kick a 33-yard field goal in the fourth quarter. The driver had been clearing yard lines on the snow-covered field throughout the day, so he was allowed on the field. But Miami protested that clearing a spot for the kicker was illegal. The officials allowed it, though.

The victory was an important one for the Patriots in the playoff race that year. Still, the Dolphins got the last laugh: They beat New England 28-13 in the first round of the postseason—in balmy Miami.

Soldier Field

Soldier Field is the home of the Chicago Bears. It is a natural-grass stadium that has a seating capacity of 61,500.

Soldier Field first was built as a World War I memorial in 1924. It re-opened after a complete renovation in 2003. The Bears have played their home games at the site since 1971 (except for 2002, when they played at the University of Illinois during the renovation).

One of the most famous games at Soldier Field was a divisional playoff between the Bears and the Philadelphia Eagles in 1988. A thick layer of fog rolled in off Lake Michigan during the second quarter and made it incredibly hard to see for fans in

■ *Greek columns loom over famous Soldier Field in Chicago.*

the stands, the media in the press box, and people watching on television. Even the players had trouble seeing passes or kicks of more than a few yards. Still, the game went on, and Chicago won, 20-12.

The annual exhibition game between the defending NFL champion and a team of college all-stars also was played at Soldier Field beginning in 1934. (The game was discontinued after 1976.) In 1947, more than 105,000 fans watched the Bears play the All-Stars.

Special Teams

The special teams are the kicking, kick-return, punt-return, and kick-coverage units of a football team. They are the players on the field for all kickoffs, punts, field goals, free kicks, and extra points (but not two-point attempts).

Starr, Bart

Bart Starr quarterbacked the Green Bay Packers to five NFL championships in 16 seasons from 1956 to 1971. The former 17th-round draft choice was inducted into the Pro Football Hall of Fame in 1977.

Starr was a cool, efficient leader and a sound decision maker. His understated manner made him something of a forgotten man in Green Bay. While playing on teams loaded with future Hall of Famers such as Paul Hornung, Jim Taylor, Jerry Kramer, Willie Wood, Ray Nitschke, and more, he probably received less recognition than a quarterback of a championship team normally would. That wasn't the case in Super Bowls I and II, however. Starr was named the most valuable player of the Packers' victories over Kansas City (35-10 in game I) and Oakland (33-14 in II).

In 16 seasons, all with Green Bay, Starr passed for 24,718 yards and 152 touchdowns. Those were Packers' records until quarterback Brett Favre came along in the 1990s and broke them. Starr has been involved in several businesses after retirement.

■ *Starr's steady play helped the Packers win.*

Staubach, Roger

Roger Staubach was the quarterback of the Dallas Cowboys' championship teams of the 1970s. His habit of rallying his team to victory from almost certain defeat earned him the nickname, "Captain Comeback."

Perhaps the most dramatic rally came in the 1972 divisional playoffs at San Francisco. After missing most of the season to injury, Staubach came off the bench in the second half. He passed for two touchdowns in the final two minutes, including the game-winner with 52 seconds left, to lift Dallas to a 30-28 victory. He was the Cowboys' starter the rest of his career, which ended in 1979.

That career didn't begin until Staubach was 27 years old in 1969. That's because the graduate of the Naval Academy spent four years in the service before joining the Cowboys. By his third season, he broke into Dallas' starting lineup, and led the team to victory in Super Bowl VI.

He also quarterbacked the club to victory in Super Bowl XII in the 1977 season. In 1979, his final year, he passed for career bests of 3,586 yards and 27 touchdowns.

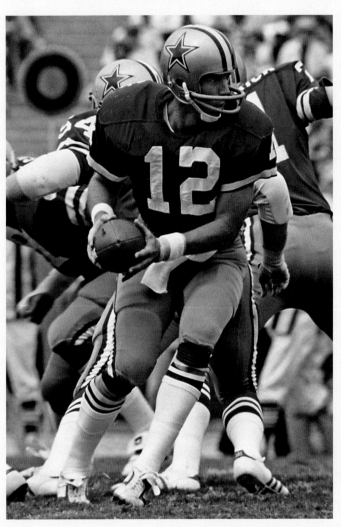

■ *Staubach ran Dallas's offense to perfection.*

The special teams don't play as a unit nearly as much as the regular offensive and defensive teams. But they can have a great effect on the outcome of a game on just a handful of plays.

Spike

A spike is a forceful throw directly into the ground. You'll see this primarily in two circumstances: by a player who has scored a touchdown and cel-

Stenerud, Jan

■ *Stenerud is the only Hall of Fame kicker.*

Jan Stenerud was the first pure kicker to make it into the Pro Football Hall of Fame. He was a member of the Class of 1991. (Before Stenerud, other kickers had made it in. But they also played other positions as well.)

It was by chance that Stenerud even began playing football. A native of Norway, he attended Montana State on a skiing scholarship. When the school's baseball coach happened to see him kicking a football around one day, he alerted the football coach, who quickly had him try out for the team.

One year later, Chiefs coach Hank Stram watched Stenerud kick 40 yard field goals in pre-game warm-ups "as if they were extra points," and Kansas City drafted him in the third round in 1966. Beginning in 1967, Stenerud played 19 NFL seasons for the Chiefs, Packers, and Vikings. He earned six AFL All-Star Game or AFC-NFC Pro Bowl nods, and kicked 373 career field goals.

ebrates in this fashion; or by a quarterback, who throws it directly in front of him immediately after taking a snap from center.

The latter is a legal and acceptable method for stopping the clock when a team is out of time outs (or to preserve a time out) in the closing seconds of a half or a game. It is considered an incomplete pass and results in a loss of down.

Spiral

Spiral is the rotation of the football as it is in flight after being thrown. A quarterback who throws a perfect spiral, or a "tight" spiral, has little wobble on his throw. The spinning motion helps the ball go farther and straighter.

A tight spiral generally is easier for the pass catcher to grab, too. The ball comes into his hands more directly and cleanly.

But the location and touch of the pass—soft or hard, lofted or on a line, as needed—are more important. Some excellent quarterbacks, such as 1950s Hall of Famer Bobby Layne, rarely threw passes that had a perfect spiral.

Spot

Simply, the spot is where the ball is placed by the officials at the conclusion of any play. It also refers to the action of "spotting" the ball. To determine the spot, watch the head linesman and line judge (see "Officials") as they race in from

Stephenson, Dwight

Dwight Stephenson played only eight seasons for the Miami Dolphins from 1980 to 1987. But in that relatively short amount of time, he established himself as one of the best centers in NFL history. In 1998, he was inducted into the Pro Football Hall of Fame.

Stephenson was a second-round draft choice out of Alabama in 1980. He broke into the Dolphins' starting lineup for good in 1982; by 1983, he earned the first of five consecutive Pro Bowl berths. He started for Miami in two Super Bowls (XVII in the 1982 season and XIX in the 1984 season). He was cut down at the height of his career by a serious knee injury suffered late in the 1987 season.

Stephenson was a powerful run blocker with tremendous quickness off the snap. But he was an effective pass blocker, too. With Stephenson anchoring the line, the Dolphins allowed fewer sacks than any other team in the league in each of his six full seasons.

■ Stephenson (57) set a new standard of excellence for centers.

the sidelines toward the middle of the field where a ball carrier is tackled. The referee or another official will place the ball based on their judgment.

"Steel Curtain"

The collective nickname given to the Pittsburgh Steelers' dominating defens-es of the 1970s. When at its best, the Steel Curtain helped carry the Steelers to back-to-back Super Bowl championships in the 1974 and 1975 seasons. Though the offense became more powerful later in the decade, the Steel Curtain also played a key role in the club's Super Bowl victories in the 1978 and 1979 seasons, too.

■ *Strahan set a single-season sack record.*

Strahan, Michael

New York Giants defensive end Michael Strahan is a dominating pass rusher who holds the NFL record for sacks in a season. His record-setting year came in 2001, when he dropped opposing quarterbacks 22.5 times, narrowly breaking the old mark of 22 set by the Jets' Mark Gastineau in 1984. Strahan's final sack, though, was controversial, when Packers quarterback Brett Favre fell to the ground without being touched.

Strahan was drafted by the Giants out of Texas Southern in the second round in 1993. By his second season, he was a full-time starter on New York's defensive line. He has posted 10 or more sacks six times in his 14-year career, and his 132.5 sacks through 2006 equaled the seventh-best mark in league history.

Strahan has made the Pro Bowl seven times, and was named the NFL's defensive player of the year for his record-setting performance in 2001.

Several members of the Steel Curtain, including defensive tackle Joe Greene, linebackers Jack Ham and Jack Lambert, and cornerback Mel Blount are members of the Pro Football Hall of Fame.

Stram, Hank

Hank Stram is a Pro Football Hall of Fame coach. He was the head coach of the Kansas City Chiefs from the inception of the franchise in 1960 (when the club was located in Dallas and known as the Texans) to 1974. He also coached the New Orleans Saints in 1976 and 1977.

Stram led the Chiefs' franchise to three championships in the 10-year history of the AFL: in 1962 (the Texans), 1966, and 1969. The 1966 Chiefs played in Super Bowl I, but lost to the NFL's Green Bay Packers. In 1969, Stram achieved the crowning moment of his career when the Chiefs upset the Minnesota Vikings 23-7 in Super Bowl IV. The Kansas City coach gained attention when NFL Films placed a microphone on him during that game. His witty remarks and enthusiastic glee over the Chiefs' victory helped make him a popular figure.

Stram was an imaginative coach whose innovations included the moving pocket for his quarterback and the two tight-end offense. Several of his Chiefs' players from the 1960s are in the Hall of Fame. Overall, his teams won 136 games in his 17 seasons as a head coach.

■ *Hank Stram led the Chiefs for 15 seasons.*

Strong Side

This is the side of the offensive line on which the tight end has lined up. Conversely, the "weak side" is the opposite side because there is one less blocker there. If a team employs a tight end on each side, or if there is no tight end on the line of scrimmage, the offensive line is balanced.

Stunt

A stunt is a planned move by two or more defensive players (usually linemen, but sometimes linebackers) who are rushing the quarterback. Instead of charging straight upfield to the quarterback like normal, one player loops behind another.

Super Bowl

The Super Bowl is the NFL's championship game. It is played annually in late January or early February between the winner of the American Football Conference (AFC) and the winner of the National Football Conference (NFC).

That is the simplest description of the Super Bowl. Nothing about the game, however, is simply put. Over its 41 years of existence, the Super Bowl has grown into an annual happening of epic proportions. In fact, it is widely considered the biggest single-day sporting event in the world.

The numbers are staggering. More than 141 million people in the United States watched the Pittsburgh Steelers and Seattle Seahawks play in Super Bowl XL in January of 2006. The big game was shown in 234 countries and territories around the world. It was broadcast in 32 different languages. The top 10 (and more) watched television programs of all time are Super Bowls…and the list goes on and on.

"The four biggest holiday celebrations in the United States are Thanksgiving, Christmas, New Year's Day, and the Super Bowl," the *Washington Post* newspaper once wrote.

The roots of the Super Bowl can be traced back to a series of secret meetings between Kansas City Chiefs owner Lamar Hunt and Dallas Cowboys executive Tex Schramm in the spring of 1966. Hunt and Schramm represented their leagues in talks to unify the two rival organizations. The two leagues' ongoing fight over players was threatening the well-being of both leagues.

Eventually—after all the necessary lawyers, league commissioners, and other executives got involved to dot all the i's and cross the t's—NFL commissioner Pete Rozelle announced on June 8, 1966, that the two leagues would become one. The marriage, which would create one league playing under the NFL name, would not take full effect until realignment and a common schedule were implemented in 1970.

In the meantime, though, the two leagues would hold a common draft and, beginning in January of 1967, send their champions to play an annual AFL-NFL World Championship Game. That was the official, if lengthy, title of the Super Bowl in its earliest years. Although some writers and fans began calling it the Super Bowl from the beginning, that name didn't become official until game III in January of 1969.

The name first came from Hunt, whose Chiefs met the Packers in game I. He got the idea from watching his young daughter play with a "Super Ball."

Roman numerals weren't used for the Super Bowl until game V. They first were

■ *Pete Rozelle's great connection: merging the NFL and AFL and creating the Super Bowl.*

utilized to avoid any confusion over dates. Super Bowl V, for instance, was played in January of 1971, but it was for the NFL championship of the 1970 season. An unintended benefit to using Roman numerals is that they added an air of importance to the game.

The winner of the Super Bowl is presented with the Vince Lombardi Trophy, shaped like a football on a tall, triangular base. It originally was called the AFL-NFL World Championship Game Trophy, but was renamed for the Hall of Fame coach following his death in 1970. Lombardi led the Packers to victory in Super Bowls I and II. The Lombardi Trophy remains in permanent possession of the winning club. A new trophy is made each year by Tiffany & Company.

The same company also makes the Pete Rozelle Trophy, which is awarded annually to the Super Bowl's most valuable player. The trophy first was named after Rozelle in game XXV in January of 1991. Rozelle served as the NFL commissioner from 1960 to 1989.

With nine games each, New Orleans and Miami have hosted the most Super Bowls. The Louisiana Superdome has hosted more games (six) than any other stadium.

85

Super Bowl I

The NFL-champion Packers had little trouble beating the AFL-champion Chiefs in the first Super Bowl. At the time, the game was called the AFL-NFL World Championship Game.

Green Bay quarterback Bart Starr, who passed for 250 yards and two touchdowns, was named the game's MVP. But wide receiver Max McGee was an unlikely hero for the Packers. McGee, a veteran who was a key player for the club's NFL champions in the early 1960s, was near the end of his career and caught only four passes while playing a limited role during the 1966 regular season. But after wide receiver Boyd Dowler

■ *Coach Lombardi celebrated after the win.*

GREEN BAY PACKERS 35, KANSAS CITY CHIEFS 10

January 15, 1967

**Los Angeles Memorial Coliseum
Los Angeles, California**

ATTENDANCE: **61,946**

Kansas City (AFL)	0	10	0	0	– 10
Green Bay (NFL)	7	7	14	7	– 35

MVP: **Bart Starr, QB, Green Bay**

HEAD COACHES
GREEN BAY: **Vince Lombardi**
KANSAS CITY: **Hank Stram**

was injured early, McGee came off the bench to catch seven passes for 138 yards. Two of his receptions went for touchdowns, including a 37-yarder to open the scoring midway through the first quarter. His second scoring grab was a 13-yard strike from Starr for a 28-10 advantage late in the third period.

The Packers led 14-10 at halftime, then broke open the game in the third quarter. The big play was safety Willie Wood's interception four plays into the second half. Wood brought back his theft 50 yards to the Chiefs' five-yard line, and Elijah Pitts ran for a touchdown on the next play. Pitts also had a one-yard touchdown run to close the scoring in the fourth quarter.

About 30,000 seats in the Los Angeles Memorial Coliseum were empty that day. It is the only Super Bowl that was not a sellout.

Super Bowl II

Quarterback Bart Starr led the Packers to their second consecutive Super Bowl victory in what was legendary coach Vince Lombardi's last game for the club. In Lombardi's nine seasons as coach, Green Bay won six conference titles and five NFL championships, plus the first two Super Bowls. (He would go on to coach one season for Washington in 1969 before his death in 1970.)

Starr was the Super Bowl MVP for the second year in a row. He completed 13 of 24 passes for 202 yards, including a 62-yard touchdown to Boyd Dowler early in the second quarter. That strike put the Packers ahead 13-0, and they remained in control the rest of the way. Although Oakland scored on a pair of 23-yard touchdown passes from Daryle Lamonica to Bill Miller, Green Bay

■ *Donny Anderson rambles against Oakland.*

otherwise kept the Raiders' high-powered passing offense in check. Lamonica completed only 15 of 34 passes and was intercepted once. Packers cornerback Herb Adderley returned that theft 60 yards for a touchdown and a 33-7 lead in the fourth quarter.

Don Chandler kicked four field goals to help keep the Packers comfortably in the lead throughout the day. His four three-pointers still shares the all-time Super Bowl record.

After the clock ticked down to zero, Packers' players carried Lombardi off the Orange Bowl field on their shoulders. "This is the best way to leave a football field," Lombardi said.

GREEN BAY PACKERS 33, OAKLAND RAIDERS 14

January 14, 1968

Orange Bowl • Miami, Florida

ATTENDANCE: 75,546

Green Bay (NFL)	3	13	10	7	— 33
Oakland (AFL)	0	7	0	7	— 14

MVP: **Bart Starr, QB, Green Bay**

HEAD COACHES
GREEN BAY: **Vince Lombardi**
OAKLAND: **John Rauch**

■ A hero QB greets his coach after the big victory.

Super Bowl III

The AFL-champion Jets beat the NFL-champion Colts in one of football's all-time stunning upsets. Baltimore entered the game as an overwhelming favorite after winning 13 of 14 games during the regular season. But New York quarterback Joe Namath brashly guaranteed a victory for his club at a luncheon during the week, then engineered the surprising win.

Matt Snell ran for 121 yards for the Jets. He capped an 80-yard drive in the second quarter with a four-yard touchdown run for the only points of the first half.

Namath led the Jets, completing 17 of 28 passes for 206 yards, and was named the game's MVP. Jim Turner kicked three field goals in the second half as the

Jets gradually increased their lead to 16-0.

The Jets' defense did the rest, keeping the Colts off the scoreboard until late in the fourth quarter. New York intercepted Baltimore quarterback Earl Morrall three times in the first half. Veteran quarterback Johnny Unitas came on and led the Colts to a touchdown with 3:19 to go, but the Jets held on to win.

New York's victory was especially important after the NFL's Packers won the first two Super Bowls so easily. The Jets gave credibility to the AFL teams that were set to join the NFL when the merger between the two leagues took full effect in 1970.

This was also the first AFL-NFL World Championship Game officially to be called the "Super Bowl."

NEW YORK JETS 16, BALTIMORE COLTS 7

January 12, 1969

Orange Bowl • Miami, Florida

ATTENDANCE: 75,389

N.Y. Jets (AFL)	0	7	6	3	— 16
Baltimore (NFL)	0	0	0	7	— 7

MVP: **Joe Namath, QB, N.Y. Jets**

HEAD COACHES
N.Y. JETS: **Weeb Ewbank**
BALTIMORE: **Don Shula**

Super Bowl IV

Quarterback Len Dawson passed for 142 yards and a touchdown to lead the Chiefs to the second consecutive upset victory by an AFL champion. Dawson became the fourth consecutive quarterback to earn the Super Bowl MVP award.

Jan Stenerud, who eventually would become the first pure kicker ever inducted into the Hall of Fame, booted three field goals to help Kansas City build a 9-0 lead in the second quarter. After the last of his field goals, a 25-yarder 7:52 before halftime, the Vikings fumbled the ensuing kickoff, and the Chiefs recovered. Six plays later, Mike Garrett's five-yard touchdown run opened up a 16-point lead for the AFL champs.

Minnesota finally scored late in the third quarter to pull within 16-7 before Kansas City put the game away the next time that it had the ball. Dawson tossed a short pass into the flat to Otis Taylor. The speedy wide receiver sprinted all the way down the sidelines to complete a 46-yard touchdown pass that was a backbreaker for the Vikings. They didn't mount a serious threat after that.

KANSAS CITY CHIEFS 23, MINNESOTA VIKINGS 7

January 11, 1970

Tulane Stadium, New Orleans, Louisiana

ATTENDANCE: **80,562**

Minnesota (NFL)	0	0	7	0 —	7
Kansas City (AFL)	3	13	7	0 —	23

MVP: **Len Dawson, QB, Kansas City**

HEAD COACHES
KANSAS CITY: **Hank Stram**
MINNESOTA: **Bud Grant**

Super Bowl IV marked the last game ever played by a team from the 10-year-old AFL. In 1970, the 10 existing AFL franchises merged into the NFL and officially became part of the established league, which split into the American and National Conferences.

Two in a row for the AFC thanks to Dawson and the Chiefs.

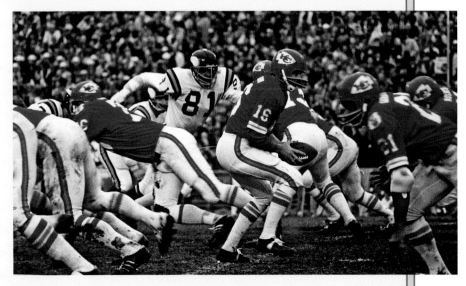

Super Bowl V

Rookie Jim O'Brien kicked a 32-yard field goal with five seconds left to lift the Colts past the Cowboys. It was the first Super Bowl played since the merger between the AFL and the NFL took full effect. Baltimore was one of three established NFL teams to join the 10 AFL teams in the newly formed American Football Conference (AFC).

Super Bowl V was an exciting game, but it was sloppy. The Colts turned over the ball seven times on four fumbles and three interceptions. But they also took away the ball four times, including a pair of key interceptions in the fourth quarter.

The Cowboys led 13-6 midway through the final period when Baltimore safety Rich Volk picked off a tipped pass from Craig Morton and returned it 30 yards to Dallas'

BALTIMORE COLTS 16, DALLAS COWBOYS 13					
January 17, 1971					
Orange Bowl • Miami, Florida					
ATTENDANCE: 79,204					
Baltimore (AFC)	0	6	0	10	— 16
Dallas (NFC)	3	10	0	0	— 13
MVP: **Chuck Howley, LB, Dallas**					
HEAD COACHES					
BALTIMORE: **Don McCafferty**					
DALLAS: **Tom Landry**					

three-yard line. Two plays later, the Colts ran it in to to tie the game at 13-13.

Later, Morton's pass was tipped again, and Baltimore linebacker Mike Curtis intercepted. His 13-yard return set up the Colts at Dallas' 28-yard line with 59 seconds to go. After two runs netted three yards, O'Brien came on for his decisive kick.

Fittingly, the game ended with another turnover. After O'Brien's field goal, the Cowboys had time for one last play. But Craig Morton's long pass was intercepted by Colts safety Jerry Logan, and time ran out.

Dallas linebacker Chuck Howley intercepted two passes and was the MVP. He was the first defensive player ever to win the award. He remains the lone player from a losing team to be so honored.

■ *The kick is up . . . O'Brien boots his game-winner.*

Super Bowl VI

After several years of coming close to winning a championship only to be denied, the Cowboys won their first NFL title with an easy victory over the Dolphins.

Quarterback Roger Staubach earned game MVP honors by passing for short touchdowns to wide receiver Lance Alworth (seven yards in the second quarter) and tight end Mike Ditka (seven yards in the fourth period). But it was the Dallas running game and defense that turned in record-setting performances.

The Cowboys utilized the two-pronged rushing attack of Duane Thomas and Walt Garrison to gain 252 yards on the ground, the most at the time in the Super Bowl's brief history. And Dallas' defense limited Miami to

■ *Two for Texas: Landry and his QB, Staubach*

only 185 total yards and three points, both Super Bowl lows at the time (the three points remains a record low). Linebacker Chuck Howley, the MVP of the Cowboys' loss in Super Bowl V, recovered a fumble and intercepted a pass to lead to 10 of his team's points.

The victory ended a string of frustration for Dallas. The Cowboys, who joined the league as an expansion team in 1960, were in the NFL Championship Game by 1966. But they lost to the Packers that year and the following season, then were ousted by Cleveland in the conference championship round in 1968 and 1969. In 1970, they lost a close decision to the Colts in Super Bowl V.

DALLAS COWBOYS 24, MIAMI DOLPHINS 3

January 16, 1972

Tulane Stadium
New Orleans, Louisiana

ATTENDANCE: 81,023

Dallas (NFC)	3	7	7	7	— 24
Miami (AFC)	0	3	0	0	— 3

MVP: **Roger Staubach, QB, Dallas**

HEAD COACHES
DALLAS: **Tom Landry**
MIAMI: **Don Shula**

Miami's defense stopped the Redskins—perfectly.

Super Bowl VII

The Dolphins capped the only perfect season in NFL history by beating the Redskins. Miami finished 17-0, winning all

MIAMI DOLPHINS 14, WASHINGTON REDSKINS 7

January 14, 1973

Los Angeles Memorial Coliseum, Los Angeles, California

ATTENDANCE: 90,182

Miami (AFC)	7	7	0	0	— 14
Washington (NFC)	0	0	0	7	— 7

MVP: **Jake Scott, S, Miami**

HEAD COACHES
MIAMI: **Don Shula**
WASHINGTON: **George Allen**

14 regular-season games and three postseason contests in just its seventh year of existence.

The Dolphins' effort in Super Bowl VII was very workmanlike. They scored two touchdowns in the first half to take a 14-0 lead at intermission, then held on for the win. The first touchdown came on Bob Griese's 28-yard pass to Howard Twilley to cap a 63-yard march. The second came on Jim Kiick's one-yard touchdown run just 18 seconds before halftime. It was set up by linebacker Nick Buoniconti's interception and 32-yard return.

Safety Jake Scott added two interceptions for Miami and was named the game's MVP. His second theft, which he returned 55 yards, came in the end zone in the fourth quarter and thwarted Washington's best drive of the game.

Moments later, Miami's Garo Yepremian lined up to kick a 42-yard field goal. The kick was blocked, though, and bounced back to Yepremian. The kicker tried to run with the ball, then tried to throw it, but fumbled it out of his hands instead. The Redskins' Mike Bass grabbed the ball in midair and raced 49 yards for a touchdown to pull his team within seven points with 2:07 to play. Washington had just one more possession after that, however, and failed to make a first down.

Super Bowl VIII

The Dolphins won their second consecutive Super Bowl by keeping the ball almost exclusively on the ground in a victory over the Vikings. Miami ran the ball on 53 of its 61 offensive plays, and gained 196 of its 259 total yards by rushing.

Bruising back Larry Csonka did most of the damage. He ran for a then-record 145 yards on 33 carries to earn game MVP honors. Csonka capped the game's opening drive, a 62-yard, 10-play march that took 5:27, by rushing five yards for a touchdown. The next time the Dolphins had the ball, they drove 56 yards in 10 more plays. This time, Jim Kiick ran one yard for the touchdown, and Miami had a 14-0 lead. It was 17-0 at halftime, and Csonka's two-yard touchdown run on the Dolphins' first possession of the third quarter put the game well out of Minnesota's reach.

Bob Griese, Miami's future Pro Football Hall of Fame quarterback, needed to pass the ball only seven times. He completed six of his attempts for 73 yards. (He also was sacked once.) All of his completions came on Dolphins' scoring drives, though. They included a 13-yard strike to Marlin Briscoe to lead to Kiick's touchdown run, and a 27-yard

MIAMI DOLPHINS 24, MINNESOTA VIKINGS 7					
January 13, 1974					
Rice Stadium • Houston, Texas					
ATTENDANCE: 71,882					
Minnesota (NFC)	0	0	0	7 —	7
Miami (AFC)	14	3	7	0 —	24
MVP: Larry Csonka, RB, Miami					
HEAD COACHES					
MIAMI: Don Shula					
MINNESOTA: Bud Grant					

pass to Paul Warfield that led to the second of Csonka's scoring runs.

Miami was the first NFL team to play in the Super Bowl three consecutive seasons. The Dolphins became the second franchise (after the Packers in games I and II) to win back-to-back Super Bowls.

■ *Miami "Zonks" in for a Super Bowl touchdown.*

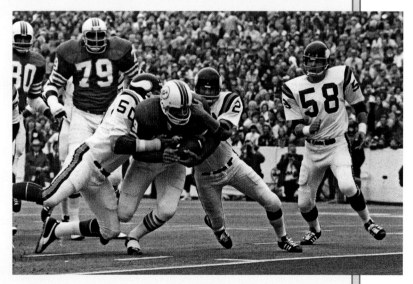

Super Bowl IX

Pittsburgh won the first championship in its four decades of existence behind its dominating "Steel Curtain" defense. That unit shut down Minnesota, allowing only 119 total yards.

Not surprisingly, Pittsburgh's defense accounted for the only scoring of the first half. Defensive end Dwight White sacked Vikings quarterback Fran Tarkenton in the end zone for a safety midway through the second period for a 2-0 lead at intermission. The Steelers then recovered a fumble on the second-half kickoff. That soon turned into a nine-yard touchdown burst by Franco Harris.

■ *Rozelle with longtime owner Art Rooney.*

PITTSBURGH STEELERS 16, MINNESOTA VIKINGS 6

January 12, 1975

**Tulane Stadium
New Orleans, Louisiana**

Attendance: 80,997

Pittsburgh (AFC)	0	2	7	7 —	16
Minnesota (NFC)	0	0	0	6 —	6

MVP: **Franco Harris, RB, Pittsburgh**

HEAD COACHES
PITTSBURGH: **Chuck Noll**
MINNESOTA: **Bud Grant**

After Minnesota pulled within three points on a blocked punt that was recovered in the end zone, Pittsburgh's offense did its share. Beginning from their 34-yard line with a little more than 10 minutes remaining, the Steelers maintained possession for six minutes and 47 seconds on an 11-play drive. The last play was Terry Bradshaw's four-yard touchdown pass to tight end Larry Brown for a 16-6 lead with just 3:31 to play. And when safety Mike Wagner intercepted Tarkenton's pass on the Vikings' next play from scrimmage, the outcome was no longer in doubt.

Pittsburgh's defense allowed Minnesota only nine first downs and 17 yards on the ground. The Steelers intercepted three of Tarkenton's passes. On offense, Harris ran for 158 yards on 34 carries to earn MVP honors.

Super Bowl X

The Steelers won their second consecutive championship in what is often considered one of the best Super Bowls ever played. Pittsburgh came from behind in the fourth quarter to win.

The Cowboys led 10-7 early in the final period before Reggie Harrison, a reserve running back for the Steelers, blocked a punt out of the end zone for a safety. That play not only pulled Pittsburgh within one point, but it also energized the Steelers and changed the game's momentum.

Pittsburgh took the ensuing free kick and quickly marched to Roy Gerela's 36-yard field goal to take the lead for the first time with 8:41 remaining in the game. Then, on Dallas' next play from scrimmage, safety Mike Wagner intercepted Roger Staubach's

■ *MVP Swann lays out for an amazing catch.*

pass, leading to another field goal. The next time they had the ball, the Steelers opened a 21-10 lead when Terry Bradshaw tossed a 64-yard touchdown pass to Lynn Swann.

That strike capped a big day for Swann, who was the game's MVP. He amassed 161 yards on just 4 receptions. One of them was a diving, juggling, 53-yard grab in the second quarter that is perhaps the most famous catch in Super Bowl history.

Wide receiver Percy Howard caught a 34-yard touchdown pass to pull the Cowboys within 21-17 with 1:48 left. Howard's achievement is noteworthy because it was the only pass that he caught in his NFL career. Dallas had one more chance after that, but Staubach's desperation pass into the end zone was intercepted by Pittsburgh safety Glen Edwards as time ran out.

PITTSBURGH STEELERS 21, DALLAS COWBOYS 17

January 18, 1976

Orange Bowl • Miami, Florida

ATTENDANCE: 80,187

Dallas (NFC)	7	3	0	7 —	17
Pittsburgh (AFC)	7	0	0	14 —	21

MVP: **Lynn Swann, WR, Pittsburgh**

HEAD COACHES
PITTSBURGH: **Chuck Noll**
DALLAS: **Tom Landry**

■ *Raiders' coach John Madden rides high.*

Super Bowl XI

Oakland extended the Vikings' misery in the Super Bowl by rolling to an easy victory. Minnesota lost for the third time in four seasons, and for the fourth time in all.

The Raiders did most of their damage on the ground, rushing for 266 of their 429 total yards. Clarence Davis gained 137 yards on just 16 carries, while Mark van Eeghen added 73 yards on 18 carries. Pete Banaszak had a pair of short touchdown runs.

Wide receiver Fred Biletnikoff was the MVP, however. He had a modest four catches

for 79 yards, but the Raiders scored touchdowns on the very next play after three of his grabs. Biletnikoff's catch early in the second quarter gave the Raiders a first-and-goal at Minnesota's one-yard line. His 17-yard catch later in the period gave them another first-and-goal at the one, and his 48-yard reception over the middle midway through the fourth quarter set up Oakland at the two.

The Vikings took to the air after falling behind 19-0 in the third quarter, and they pulled within 12 points when Fran Tarkenton tossed an eight-yard touchdown pass to Sammy White in the final minute of the period. But they couldn't get any closer than that. The Raiders' defense made sure of it by intercepting Tarkenton twice in the fourth quarter. Cornerback Willie Brown returned the second theft 75 yards for a touchdown to make it 32-7 with 5:43 left.

OAKLAND RAIDERS 32, MINNESOTA VIKINGS 14

January 9, 1977

Rose Bowl • Pasadena, California

ATTENDANCE: 103,438

Oakland (AFC)	0	16	3	13 —	32
Minnesota (NFC)	0	0	7	7 —	14

MVP: **Fred Biletnikoff, WR, Oakland**

HEAD COACHES
OAKLAND: **John Madden**
MINNESOTA: **Bud Grant**

Super Bowl XII

The Broncos won their first AFC championship behind their "Orange Crush" defense, but it was the Cowboys who made the big plays on defense in the Super Bowl. They forced eight turnovers and posted four sacks en route to an easy victory.

Defensive end Harvey Martin (an end) and Randy White (a tackle) led the Cowboys' relentless assault on Denver quarterbacks; the pair shared MVP honors. Denver's Craig Morton, who played for Dallas' Super Bowl champions in the 1971 season, started and completed only 4 of 15 passes for 39 yards and was intercepted four times. The first led to Dallas running back Tony Dorsett's three-yard touchdown run to open the scoring.

Just two plays later, cornerback Aaron Kyle picked off Morton's pass and returned it 19 yards to Denver's 35-yard line. Efren Herrera soon kicked a 35-yard field goal to make it 10-0, and the Cowboys remained in control the rest of the way.

Dallas didn't need much offense while limiting the Broncos to only 156 total yards. The Cowboys did have a pair of highlight-reel plays on that side of the ball, though.

In the third quarter, wide receiver Butch Johnson made a spectacular, diving, fingertip grab of a pass from Roger Staubach to complete a 45-yard touchdown play.

DALLAS COWBOYS 27, DENVER BRONCOS 10

January 15, 1978

**Louisiana Superdome
New Orleans, Louisiana**

Attendance: 75,583

Dallas (NFC)	10	3	7	7 –	27
Denver (AFC)	0	0	10	0 –	10

MVP: **Harvey Martin, DE, Dallas and Randy White, DT, Dallas**

**HEAD COACHES
DALLAS: Tom Landry
DENVER: Red Miller**

In the fourth quarter, fullback Robert Newhouse took a handoff from Staubach and tossed a 29-yard touchdown pass to wide receiver Golden Richards. That capped the day's scoring with 7:04 left.

■ *Dynamite Dallas duo: White and Martin*

Pro Football Hall of Fame Members

NOTE: *Years listed include only those years with an NFL (or 1960-69 AFL) team.*

Positions abbreviations: C–center; CB–cornerback; DB–defensive back; DE–defensive end; DT–defensive tackle; E–end; FB–fullback; FL–flanker; G–guard; HB–halfback; K–kicker; LB–linebacker; P–punter; QB–quarterback; RB–running back; S–safety; T–tackle; TE–tight end; WR–wide receiver.

A

Herb Adderley, CB (1961-1972)

Troy Aikman, QB (1989-2000)

George Allen, Coach (1966-1977)

Marcus Allen, RB (1982-1997)

■ *CB Mel Blount won four Super Bowls.*

Lance Alworth, WR (1962-1972)

Doug Atkins, DE (1953-1969)

B

Morris (Red) Badgro, E (1927-28, 1930-36)

Lem Barney, CB (1967-1977)

Cliff Battles, HB (1932-37)

Sammy Baugh, QB (1937-1952)

Chuck Bednarik, C-LB (1949-1962)

Bert Bell, Team owner-Commissioner
    (1933-1959)

Bobby Bell, LB (1963-1974)

Raymond Berry, E (1955-1967)

Elvin Bethea, DE (1968-1983)

Charles W. Bidwill, Sr., Team owner
    (1933-1947)

Fred Biletnikoff, WR (1965-1978)

George Blanda, QB-K (1949-1958,
    1960-1975)

Mel Blount, CB (1970-1983)

Terry Bradshaw, QB (1970-1983)

Bob (Boomer) Brown, T (1964-1973)

Jim Brown, FB (1957-1965)

Paul Brown, Coach (1950-1962, 1968-1975)

Roosevelt Brown, T (1953-1965)

Willie Brown, CB (1963-1978)

Junious (Buck) Buchanan, DT (1963-1975)

Nick Buoniconti, LB (1962-1974, 1976)

Dick Butkus, LB (1965-1973)

C

Earl Campbell, RB (1978-1985)

Tony Canadeo, HB (1941-44, 1946-1952)

Joe Carr, NFL president (1921-1939)

Harry Carson, LB (1976-1988)

Dave Casper, TE (1974-1984)

Guy Chamberlin, E-Coach (1920-28)

Jack Christiansen, S (1951-58)

Earl (Dutch) Clark, QB (1931-32, 1934-38)

George Connor, T-LB (1948-1955)

Jimmy Conzelman, QB-Coach-Owner
   (1920-1930, 1940-42, 1946-48)

Lou Creekmur, T-G (1950-59)

Larry Csonka, RB (1968-1974, 1976-79)

D

Al Davis, Team and league administrator
   (1963-2007)

Willie Davis, DE (1958-1969)

Len Dawson, QB (1957-1975)

Joe DeLamielleure, G (1973-1985)

Eric Dickerson, RB (1983-1993)

Dan Dierdorf, T (1971-1983)

Mike Ditka, TE (1961-1972)

Art Donovan, DT (1950-1961)

Tony Dorsett, RB (1977-1988)

John (Paddy) Driscoll, QB (1920-29)

Bill Dudley, HB (1942, 1945-1951, 1953)

■ *John Elway was famed for his escape ability.*

E

Albert Glen (Turk) Edwards, T (1932-1940)

Carl Eller, DE (1964-1979)

John Elway, QB (1983-1998)

Weeb Ewbank, Coach (1954-1973)

F

Tom Fears, E (1948-1956)

Jim Finks, Administrator (1964-1982,
   1986-1993)

Ray Flaherty, Coach (1936-1942)

Len Ford, DE (1950-58)

Dan Fortmann, G (1936-1943)

Dan Fouts, QB (1973-1987)

Benny Friedman, QB (1927-1934)

G

Frank Gatski, C (1950-57)

Bill George, LB (1952-1966)

Joe Gibbs, Coach (1981-1992, 2005-06)

Frank Gifford, HB-FL (1952-1960, 1962-64)

Sid Gillman, Coach (1955-1969, 1971, 1973-74)

Otto Graham, QB (1950-55)

■ *Pro football's first superstar: Red Grange.*

Harold (Red) Grange, HB (1925, 1927, 1929-1934)

Bud Grant, Coach (1967-1983, 1985)

Joe Greene, DT (1969-1981)

Forrest Gregg, T (1956, 1958-1971)

Bob Griese, QB (1967-1980)

Lou Groza, T-K (1950-59, 1961-67)

Joe Guyon, HB (1920-25, 1927)

H

George Halas, E-Coach-Owner (1920-1983)

Jack Ham, LB (1971-1982)

Dan Hampton, DT-DE (1979-1990)

John Hannah, G (1973-1985)

Franco Harris, RB (1972-1984)

Mike Haynes, CB (1976-1989)

Ed Healey, T (1920-27)

Mel Hein, C (1931-1945)

Ted Hendricks, LB (1969-1983)

Wilbur (Pete) Henry, T (1920-23, 1925-28)

Arnie Herber, QB (1930-1940, 1944-45)

Bill Hewitt, E (1932-39, 1943)

Gene Hickerson, G (1958-1973)

Clarke Hinkle, FB (1932-1941)

Elroy (Crazylegs) Hirsch, HB-E (1949-1957)

Paul Hornung, HB (1957-1962, 1964-66)

Ken Houston, S (1967-1980)

Robert (Cal) Hubbard, T (1927-1933, 1935-36)

Sam Huff, LB (1956-1967, 1969)

Lamar Hunt, Team owner (1960-2006)

Don Hutson, E (1935-1945)

I

Michael Irvin, WR (1988-1999)

J

Jimmy Johnson, CB (1961-1976)

John Henry Johnson, FB (1954-1966)

Charlie Joiner, WR (1969-1986)

David (Deacon) Jones, DE (1961-1974)

Stan Jones, G-DT (1954-1966)

Henry Jordan, DT (1957-1969)

Sonny Jurgensen, QB (1957-1974)

K

Jim Kelly, QB (1986-1996)

Leroy Kelly, RB (1964-1973)

Walt Kiesling, G-Coach (1926-1944, 1954-56)

Frank (Bruiser) Kinard, T (1938-1944)

Paul Krause, S (1964-1979)

L

Earl (Curly) Lambeau, Coach (1920-1953)

Jack Lambert, LB (1974-1984)

Tom Landry, Coach (1960-1988)

Dick (Night Train) Lane, CB (1952-1965)

Jim Langer, C (1970-1981)

Willie Lanier, LB (1967-1977)

Steve Largent, WR (1976-1989)

Yale Lary, DB-P (1952-53, 1956-1964)

Dante Lavelli, E (1950-56)

Bobby Layne, QB (1948-1962)

Alphonse (Tuffy) Leemans, FB (1936-1943)

Marv Levy, Coach (1978-1982, 1986-1997)

Bob Lilly, DT (1961-1974)

Larry Little, G (1967-1980)

James Lofton, WR (1978-1993)

Vince Lombardi, Coach (1959-1967, 1969)

Howie Long, DE (1981-1993)

Ronnie Lott, CB-S (1981-1994)

Sid Luckman, QB (1939-1950)

William Roy (Link) Lyman, T (1922-28, 1930-31, 1933-34)

M

Tom Mack, G (1966-1978)

John Mackey, TE (1963-1972)

John Madden, Coach (1969-1978)

Tim Mara, Team owner (1925-1959)

Wellington Mara, Owner (1937-2006)

Gino Marchetti, DE (1952-1964, 1966)

Dan Marino, QB (1983-1999)

George Preston Marshall, Owner (1932-1969)

Ollie Matson, HB (1952, 1954-1966)

Bruce Matthews, G-T-C (1983-2001)

Don Maynard, WR (1958, 1960-1973)

George McAfee, HB (1940-41, 1945-1950)

Mike McCormack, T (1951, 1954-1962)

Tommy McDonald, WR (1957-1968)

Hugh McElhenny, HB (1952-1964)

John (Blood) McNally, HB (1925-1938)

Mike Michalske, G (1927-1935, 1937)

Wayne Millner, E (1936-1941, 1945)

Bobby Mitchell, RB-WR (1958-1968)

Ron Mix, T (1960-69, 1971)

Joe Montana, QB (1979-1994)

Warren Moon, QB (1984-2000)

Lenny Moore, FL-RB (1956-1967)

Marion Motley, FB (1950-53, 1955)

Mike Munchak, G (1982-1993)

Anthony Muñoz, T (1980-1992)

George Musso, G-T (1933-1944)

N

Bronko Nagurski, FB (1930-37, 1943)

Joe Namath, QB (1965-1977)

Earle (Greasy) Neale, Coach (1941-1950)

Ernie Nevers, FB (1926-27, 1929-1931)

Ozzie Newsome, TE (1978-1990)

Ray Nitschke, LB (1958-1972)

Chuck Noll, Coach (1969-1991)

Leo Nomellini, DT (1950-1963)

O

Merlin Olsen, DT (1962-1976)

Jim Otto, C (1960-1974)

Steve Owen, Tackle-Coach (1924-1953)

P

Alan Page, DT (1967-1981)

Clarence (Ace) Parker, QB (1937-1941, 1945)

Jim Parker, G-T (1957-1967)

Walter Payton, RB (1975-1987)

Joe Perry, FB (1950-1963)

Pete Pihos, E (1947-1955)

Fritz Pollard, HB-Coach (1920-23, 1925-26)

R

Hugh (Shorty) Ray, Supervisor of officials (1938-1952)

Dan Reeves, Team owner (1941-1971)

Mel Renfro, CB-S (1964-1977)

John Riggins, RB (1971-79, 1981-85)

Jim Ringo, C (1953-1967)

Andy Robustelli, DE (1951-1964)

Art Rooney, Team owner (1933-1988)

Dan Rooney, Team owner (1955-2007)

Pete Rozelle, Commissioner (1960-1989)

S

Bob St. Clair, T (1953-1963)

Barry Sanders, RB (1989-1998)

Charlie Sanders, TE (1968-1977)

Gale Sayers, RB (1965-1971)

Joe Schmidt, LB (1953-1965)

Tex Schramm, Team president-general manager (1947-1956, 1960-1989)

Lee Roy Selmon, DE (1976-1984)

Billy Shaw, G (1961-69)

Art Shell, T (1968-1982)

Don Shula, Coach (1963-1995)

O.J. Simpson, RB (1969-1979)

Mike Singletary, LB (1981-1992)

Jackie Slater, T (1976-1995)

Jackie Smith, TE (1963-1978)

John Stallworth, WR (1974-1987)

Bart Starr, QB (1956-1971)

Roger Staubach, QB (1969-1979)

Ernie Stautner, DT (1950-1963)

Jan Stenerud, K (1967-1985)

Dwight Stephenson, C (1980-87)

Hank Stram, Coach (1960-1974, 1976-77)

Ken Strong, HB (1929-1935, 1939, 1944-47)

Joe Stydahar, T (1936-1942, 1945-46)

Lynn Swann, WR (1974-1982)

T

Fran Tarkenton, QB (1961-1978)

Charley Taylor, RB-WR (1964-1975, 1977)

Jim Taylor, FB (1958-1967)

Lawrence Taylor, LB (1981-1993)

Thurman Thomas, RB (1988-2000)

Jim Thorpe, HB (1920-26, 1928)

Y.A. Tittle, QB (1950-1964)

George Trafton, C (1920-1932)

Charley Trippi, HB-QB (1947-1955)

Emlen Tunnell, S (1948-1961)

Clyde (Bulldog) Turner, C (1940-1952)

U

Johnny Unitas, QB (1956-1973)

Gene Upshaw, G (1967-1981)

V

Norm Van Brocklin, QB (1949-1960)

Steve Van Buren, HB (1944-1951)

W

Doak Walker, HB (1950-55)

Bill Walsh, Coach (1979-1988)

Paul Warfield, WR (1964-1977)

Bob Waterfield, QB (1945-1952)

Mike Webster, C (1974-1990)

Roger Wehrli, CB (1969-1982)

Arnie Weinmeister, DT (1950-53)

Randy White, DT (1975-1988)

Reggie White, DE-DT (1985-1998, 2000)

Dave Wilcox, LB (1964-1974)

Bill Willis, G (1950-53)

Larry Wilson, S (1960-1972)

■ *Johnny Unitas: The ultimate QB as leader*

Kellen Winslow, TE (1979-1987)

Alex Wojciechowicz, C (1938-1950)

Willie Wood, S (1960-1971)

Rayfield Wright, T (1967-1979)

Y

Ron Yary, T (1968-1982)

Steve Young, QB (1985-1999)

Jack Youngblood, DE (1971-1984)

*Read the index this way: "**4**:62" means Volume 4, page 62.*

National Football League

NOTE: *The numbers following a team's name indicate the volume and page number where the information can be found. "I:36" means Volume I, page 36.*

American Football Conference

East Division		North Division		South Division		West Division	
Buffalo Bills	I:36	Baltimore Ravens	I:24	Houston Texans	II:16	Denver Broncos	I:64
Miami Dolphins	II:70	Cincinnati Bengals	I:50	Indianapolis Colts	II:24	Kansas City Chiefs	II:38
New England Patriots	II:86	Cleveland Browns	I:54	Jacksonville Jaguars	II:32	Oakland Raiders	III:4
New York Jets	II:92	Pittsburgh Steelers	III:28	Tennessee Titans	IV:62	San Diego Chargers	III:56

National Football Conference

East Division		North Division		South Division		West Division	
Dallas Cowboys	I:58	Chicago Bears	I:46	Atlanta Falcons	I:20	Arizona	I:14
New York Giants	II:90	Detroit Lions	I:66	Carolina Panthers	I:42	St. Louis	III:54
Philadelphia Eagles	III:24	Green Bay Packers	I:100	New Orleans Saints	II:88	San Francisco	III:58
Washington Redskins	IV:90	Minnesota Vikings	II:74	Tampa Bay Buccaneers	IV:54	Seattle	III:66

About the Authors

James Buckley Jr. is the author of more than 60 books for young readers on a wide variety of topics—mostly sports! He has written several books on football, including *Eyewitness Football*, *Eyewitness Super Bowl*, and *America's Greatest Game*. Formerly with *Sports Illustrated* and NFL Publishing, he is now the president of the Shoreline Publishing Group, which produced these volumes.

Jim Gigliotti was a senior editor at NFL Publishing and the editor of the league's national GameDay program. He has written hundreds of articles on football for many magazines and Web sites, as well as several children's books on other sports topics.

Matt Marini was also an editor with NFL Publishing, where he oversaw the *NFL Record & Fact Book* among many other writing and editing duties.

John Wiebusch is one of America's leading experts on pro football. As the vice president and creative director of NFL Publishing, he was the editor of the Super Bowl program for 32 years, and author and/or editor of thousands of articles on all aspects of pro football. John is the author of *Lombardi* as well as dozens of other books, and has edited more than 200 titles. He also wrote a popular NFL history column on AOL. He contributed numerous essays on Hall of Fame personalities in these volumes.